SECRETS OF WINNING
POST PLAY BASKETBALL

SECRETS OF WINNING
POST PLAY BASKETBALL

Rich Grawer

Parker Publishing Company, Inc., West Nyack, N.Y.

© 1980 by

Parker Publishing Company, Inc.
West Nyack, New York

Library of Congress Cataloging in Publication Data

Grawer, Rich
  Secrets of winning post play basketball.

  Includes index.
  1. Basketball coaching.   I. Title.
GV885.3.G7   796.32'32   80-15372
ISBN 0-13-798751-X

Printed in the United States of America

HOW THIS BOOK WILL HELP YOUR POST PLAY

Basketball has entered an era of highly specialized and scientific play, catapulting to the forefront the utmost importance of the complete team. One phase of complete team basketball is the play of the center, the pivot, or the player or players who are primarily in the key. This book shares those coaching secrets about post play that have helped me develop a winning program.

The successful coach does not win with chance, with prayers, or with hopes. He wins because he is prepared for every situation, because he has covered every phase of the game as thoroughly as possible in practice. He wins because he has taught the game effectively. He has taught his players individual skills and also how to play together as a team.

The outcome of most basketball games is determined by what goes on in what I call the "multi-purpose area"—the key. This is usually the stomping ground, the domain, of the player that we call the POST MAN, THE PIVOT, or THE CENTER. No team wins unless it employs a capable athlete in this position and unless it utilizes this particular area on the court—the area of the key. Even those teams employing a passing game still flash players into this area.

Many will argue that you need a 6'7 or 6'8 pivot man to win championships. I cannot deny that this helps. We won a state championship with a 6'10 post man, but we also won a state title with a 6'4 post man and reached the state quarterfinals with a 6'1 post man. Good, intelligent, programmed post play is far more important than the size of the post player in winning championships.

We have an organized, definite program for our post players. That program is outlined and explained *in its entirety* in this book. The off-season training, the physical development, the physical skills, the mental aspects of post play, the techniques of post play and then the various offenses that we use to utilize the post player that we have developed—all of this is contained in the book.

Many books are written and clinics given on a particular offense. We let our players determine our offense, and particularly, our POST PLAYER. How to analyze your personnel and then use them is one

5

of the most delicate skills in coaching. The first seven chapters of this book are devoted to the PLAYER and the POSITION. The next four chapters are devoted to team offenses and ideas that allow the post man to best maximize the specific skills and techniques of his position. And the final four chapters emphasize specialty situations, including defense, practice secrets and evaluation hints.

Every high school coach can benefit by these techniques. High school coaches have little control over the talent they get. They can't recruit or give scholarships. Sometimes we are blessed with the tall, talented post man. Other times, most often, not. But I firmly believe that intelligent use of the post player can and will win many games, no matter the size of that player. An offense has to use the multi-purpose area of the court—the key. How to operate in this area INDIVIDUALLY and as a TEAM is what this book is all about.

A solid team builds a offense from the inside out. This means developing the good, inside game by getting the most out of your post man. Obviously, a physically strong and mentally tough player must roam the key. How does one acquire this strength? This book enumerates the exercises, the physical training, most beneficial to upper body strength, leg development, and overall endurance. It also explains and diagrams drills to improve quickness and jumping ability.

Too often, as coaches, we take for granted such fundamental concepts as "catching the ball" or "giving a target" or "reading the defensive center." The winning coach leaves nothing to chance, takes nothing for granted. This book systematically shows you how to teach positioning, giving a proper target, catching the ball, reading the defense, and moving after receiving the ball. The book runs the whole gamut of skills and techniques to be mastered by the post man from protecting the ball to conversion to defense.

Your post player should be your leading rebounder and one of your best passers. *Secrets of Winning Post Play Basketball* describes the development of the post player's efficiency in both passing and rebounding. It shows also the drills necessary to improve positioning, lateral movement to both sides of the boards, and power moves inside. The book reveals secrets on how to improve the post man's outlet passing and passes to the weak side—two of the most important types of passes that the post man needs to master in order to be effective.

Having mastered individual techniques and skills, the post man then needs to be placed into the proper offense to maximize his use of these skills. Have you thought about a SHUFFLE type offense for a small, quick post man? What about a LOW POST POWER offense for the big, but rather slow post man? Or a HI-LOW offense for a versatile post man or two post men? What type of post man fits best into a PASSING GAME or MOTION OFFENSE? And what about ZONE OFFENSES? This book gives you ideas and programs on these questions that have proven effective. You must be able to integrate the post man into your system or alter your system to fit your post man.

There can be no greater thrill in coaching than to see your post man—the hub of your team—on the hardwood, playing with the grace and fluidity that you have brought out in him. To see your team win with good percentage shots, to see your team perform well in the "multi-purpose" area because of programmed post play is sheer coaching delight. I wish there were an easy way to accomplish this. There is no short-cut. Time, hard work, and dedication are the only answers. The players and the coach must be willing to spend hours working together on specific skills and techniques. And the player himself must work countless hours alone in order to accomplish all that the coach has outlined for him. This book will aid player and coach in post play development during the season but also during the post and pre-season.

Remember: the game is won in the key, the multi-purpose area. Have you developed the player that you will use in that area to his and your maximum? If you have never been exposed to a detailed, well-planned program for your player, this book will be especially valuable.

Rich Grawer

CONTENTS

1

THE IMPORTANCE
OF POST PLAY

THE MULTI-PURPOSE AREA AND PLAYER

Many basketball games are won or lost because of the play in what I call the "multi-purpose" area of the court. This multi-purpose area is basically the key—including the area above the free line to the top of the circle (Diagram 1.1). The team that gets the ball into this area the most, the team that controls this area both offensively and defensively, will be the one that wins the game.

Coaches must realize the importance of getting the ball inside. It is like establishing your running game in football so that you can eventually pass. If you don't put the ball into the multi-purpose area and establish some kind of superiority in this area, then your perimeter people will never get that uncontested, unmolested 15-18 foot jumper.

Besides the obvious advantage of getting a good shot when the ball is put into the multi-purpose area, this is an excellent area from which to pass. From the high-post, free-throw area, many scoring opportunities are opened for cutters streaking inside or perimeter players steppping into open gaps of sagging defenses. See Diagram 1.2.

One of the best ways to defeat the zone is to make the defense tilt to one side, hitting the post player with a pass and then countering the zone with a quick pass to the opposite side. See Diagrams 1.3, 1.4, and 1.5.

This area is also an excellent spot on the court from which to dribble penetrate to the hole. A lot of things happen when this occurs opening excellent passing and cutting lanes, many free throw opportunities and good rebound opportunities as the defense reacts to the driver.

Any shot taken from this multi-purpose area lends itself to good rebounding positioning by the offense. See Diagram 1.6. More will be said about rebounding in a later chapter. Let it suffice for now to say that a shot taken from the multi-purpose area has many more good rebounding opportunities than one taken from the corner or sides. Let it also suffice for now to say that the "multi-purpose area" of the court is the area where "THINGS HAPPEN."

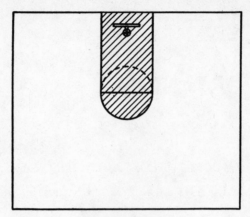

Diagram 1.1

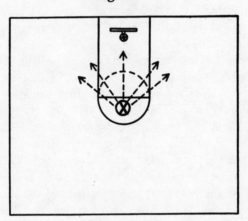

Diagram 1.2

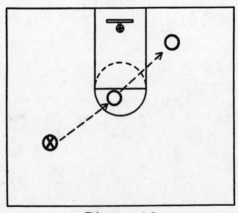

Diagram 1.3

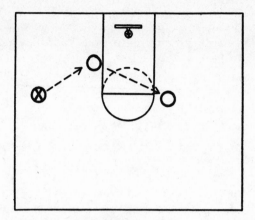

Diagram 1.4

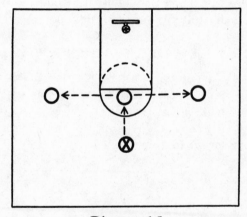

Diagram 1.5

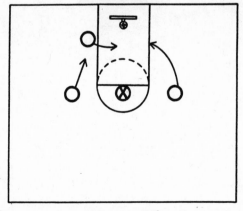

Diagram 1.6

With this in mind, it should be obvious that a coach needs a very capable athlete to play the multi-purpose area. Too often coaches stick a tall, gangly kid—weak physically—in other words, a poor athlete—in this area. This stifles much offensive initiative. It is our philosophy to play one of our better athletes here, whether he be tall or not. The type of player who should man this area should be a good athlete; he should be able to pass the basketball. He should be a master of body control. He should be active and able to get to the boards. And finally, he should be able to master a few simple shots—the layup, the short hook, and inside power moves.

This player need not be your tallest; though, if a tall player would exhibit the characteristics described above, he would be the ideal man for that spot. But this player must be intelligent. He is the hub of the offense. Height, quickness, and great shooting ability need not be there. But know-how, movement, ability to pass, rebound and outlet, and some ability to hit the inside shot are a must.

THEORIES ON USING THE POST PLAYER

In analyzing play in the multi-purpose area, you should decide exactly how you wish to use the post man. Do you want the post man to be basically a high post player? Do you want to use the player exclusively at the low or middle post? Designations of high, middle, and low post are shown in Diagram 1.7.

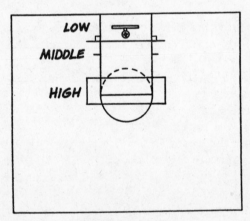

Diagram 1.7

Perhaps you want to let the post man "roam"—high, low, out on the baseline, step off to the wing, or do you want an open system in order to run different people in and out of the multi-purpose area, thereby hoping to create confusion on the part of the defense? Many motion or passing game offenses employ this method. Do you wish˙to employ two post men—high-low? These are just a few of the questions that only you, the coach, can answer. To solve these problems and answer these questions, you must analyze your personnel and determine the type of team that you wish to mold.

We have a general idea or philosophy on what type of team we want. We usually want to run and attack quickly, putting pressure on the defense. We like to release a guard from the defensive end on the shot and run the ball up court whether after a rebound or a made field goal. BUT, we always adjust this philosophy to our personnel and PARTICULARLY to the person that we will designate as the player to operate in the multi-purpose area.

With a small post man, 6'1 and under, we continue to run and try to create many more full court opportunities for our squad. We figure that it would be a disadvantage for us to play half court with the opposition when we have a small man operating in the multi-purpose area. We will usually start a small post man at the high-post, free-throw line area. With a tall post player, we generally keep him at the mid or low areas. With an in-between sized post man—6'3 - 6'4— with some ability—we would like him to be able to roam anywhere along the multi-purpose area. With a small team at all five positions, we will run people in and out. This latter involves a lot more teaching time, as the coach has to school every player in the techniques and art of posting up.

To help convey the idea that that multi-purpose area of the court is so important to winning, we run a drill that we call "MARINE BASKETBALL-NO DRIBBLE." Any number of players can participate —as long as they are divided equally into two teams. Since we have 14 players on our roster, we play 7 on 7. There is no dribble allowed in this drill. The idea is to PASS the ball into the multi-purpose area or some part of the multi-purpose area and thereby score a point for your team. When the passed ball is caught by a teammate with *both feet* in the designated area, 1 point is scored for that team. Remember, players cannot dribble. They must advance the ball up court against the defense by passing and cutting. Players must move constantly, meet their pass, and keep their head up for an opening into a player in the multi-purpose area. It is not as easy as it sounds. The defense is encouraged to vary coverage—tight man, sagging man (sag around the multi-purpose area full court pressing, denial in the passing lanes, and so on. Once a team has passed the ball into the multi-purpose area, it goes on defense. The offense has to take the ball out of bounds and advance it upcourt via the passing route. Full court pressure defense is allowed. However, you call all obvious fouls and award a point to the team fouled. All violations—traveling, offensive foul, 3-second—are called and the defensive team takes the ball out of bounds. The activity is lots of fun and does serve to teach and emphasize many important concepts that deal with the game of basketball—the most important of which (for our purpose) are the emphasis on the post play of the multi-purpose player and the emphasis upon the other players of looking to this area and getting the ball inside.

As variations to this game, limit each team to one or two specific players who can go into the designated area. They have to free themselves, and the team can score only when they have caught the pass in this area with both feet completely inside the area. Other times narrow or shrink the multi-purpose area to (A) the circle, (B) below the foul line, (C) only above the foul line. Now, only by passing the ball to a teammate in the specific area can the offensive team gain one point. The time that you have available and the quality and character of your players should determine the length of the contest. A time limit can be set or 10-12 points can be the goal. In our case, our players are so good at it and the defense so rugged, that we usually go to a designated time limit. This makes for a good game and still gives us the passing, cutting, emphasizing of the importance of the multi-purpose area and conditioning that we hope to achieve by the drill.

THE DeSMET SYSTEM

As mentioned before, we have run the gamut of post players—from the 6'1 kid to the 6'11 player. Therefore, we have run different offenses to suit the player and his skills. However, our philosophy about post play hasn't changed. Our theory of getting the ball inside to a player who does know how to operate effectively has not changed with the size of ability of the post man.

Every player who is going to play out of the multi-purpose area is required to listen to a forty-five minute cassette tape which I have made on the importance of post play and the importance of the player in the multi-purpose area. The tape contains many of the major points that are in this book—techniques of posting up, giving a proper target, offensive moves after catching the ball, passing, and the like. It also contains some important psychological points that everyone who operates in this area must realize. The tape emphasizes the importance of the post man as the hub of the team. It stresses the importance of the post man to every phase of our game—offense, defense, out of bounds plays, delay, screening, and others. It reminds the post man that if he'll give the ball back to the open man, the other players will more willingly pass the ball inside to him. It emphasizes to the post man that he will NOT be given a single pass unless he has a target hand and arm up. And it states emphatically that players will not be scolded or yanked from the game for a bad pass made to the post area. We hope, in this way, to encourage all players to look inside and try to get the ball into the multi-purpose area.

The player is constantly reminded on the tape that players will readily pass the ball inside if they know they will get it back. This spells T-E-A-M play, and our post player, though he knows that he is the hub of our attack, knows also that the team come first.

Besides making our post player listen to the tape, we also make him or them take notes on it and show these to the coaching staff. This, we hope, will make the post player know PHILOSOPHICALLY what we expect from him. If a player doesn't know or understand what you are trying to teach and do, he will never be able to do it. So, we believe that these forms of communication—the tape recording and the subsequent note-taking—better prepare our multi-purpose player for the actual on the court work that comes later.

2

OFF-SEASON AND PRE-SEASON CONDITIONING FOR THE POST PLAYER

It is a rarity to have any high school player with all of the skills we would like to see in an athlete. Rarely, if ever, do we get a chance to coach the complete player—the real blue chipper.

In ranking the techniques and skills that we would like post players to have, we have realistically come up with five. I say "realistically" because we know that we cannot teach a youngster everything. Certain skills and techniques are harder to teach and harder to master than others. Thus, we emphasize five:

1. Strength and agility,
2. Ability to pass.
3. Ability to rebound and outlet.
4. Ability to hit the inside shot (power and short hook).
5. Basketball recognition: read defenses and see open people.

You will notice that there are some obvious basketball skills missing from our list: jumping, dribbling, cutting, quickness, and others. This is not to say that we don't try to develop these in our post men. However, with limited time and necessary attention that must be given to the other players and to team concepts, it is often mandatory for us to emphasize some skills or techniques over others. And through the years, we have determined that these five are most important for our post men.

Our off-season and pre-season training for the post man centers around these two: #1—strength and agility; #4—inside shooting. By the time our official practice season begins near the first of November, we want our post man to have worked especially hard on his strength, agility, and inside game. We can emphasize the others in our practice sessions.

OFF-SEASON PROGRAM

All of our players report to me after the official end of our season in March. I give them a written evaluation form, citing their strengths, weaknesses, and areas of concentration for the summer months. Here is a sample evaluation form. (See pages 20 and 21).

In all cases where we rate the player a #3 (average) or below, we take great pains to specifically outline particular drills and excercises that he can do to improve on that skill. Too often we coaches criticize but don't suggest ways to improve.

Our post man at this time receives his OFF-SEASON PROGRAM. He is asked to work four days a week minimum. We ask all players to keep a chart of their workout and to write to the coach once every two weeks with a copy of the workout chart. Let me emphasize that the purpose of this written letter is not really to check up on the players. We have built such a winning tradition that our players WANT to work and literally cry out for things to do in the area of basketball. But the main purpose of the letter is to develop a sense of responsibility in our youngsters and to develop some feeling of rapport between the player and the coach. I might add that I write to them also and don't even mention basketball in most of the letters.

Stretching

The OFF-SEASON PROGRAM begins with 5-10 minutes of stretching. We begin all official practices with stretching and flexibility. It has really cut down on our injuries. We include the following exercises (the arrows point to those areas of the body where you will most likely feel the stretch.)

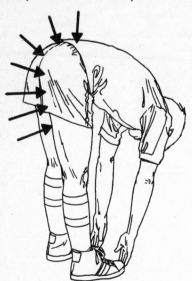

From a standing position, feet shoulder width apart, slowly bend forward at the waist. Relax and feel an easy stretch in the back of your legs or hamstrings. Hold stretch for 20 seconds. As you progress with this, you should be able to extend the arms farther and farther, ultimately placing the palms of the hands on the floor (Diagram 2.1).

Diagram 2.1

BASKETBALL EVALUATION—INDIVIDUAL PLAYER

Player's name: _____ Yr. in school_____

Address: _____ Phone_____

Parent's Name: _____ Ht. _____Wt._____

Vertical Jump_____ Grade Point Ave. _____ Class rank_____

*****THE MOST IMPORTANT TIME IN BASKETBALL IS BETWEEN MARCH-SEPTEMBER*****

Date of evaluation_____

Rating Scale: 1. EXCELLENT
                2. GOOD
                3. AVERAGE
                4. POOR
                5. NEED TO START FROM SCRATCH

DEFENSIVE ABILITY

A. STANCE   _____

B. FOOTWORK   _____

C. HUSTLE/DESIRE   _____

D. ON THE BALL   _____

E. OFF THE BALL   _____

F. REBOUNDING   _____

G. OVERALL   _____

BALL-HANDLING ABILITY

A. PASSING   _____

B. DRIBBLING   _____

C. SEEING OPEN MAN _____

D. PRESSURE OPEN MAN _____

E. OVERALL   _____

SHOOTING ABILITY

A. FORM   _____

B. FREE THROWS   _____

C. SHOT SELECTION _____

D. WILLINGNESS
    TO WORK   _____

E. OVERALL   _____

OFFENSIVE MOVES

    A. TRIPLE THREAT POSITION _____
    B. STATIONARY MOVES   _____
    C. MOVES ON DRIBBLE   _____
    D. ABILITY TO SCREEN   _____
    E. RECOGNIZE BREAK   _____
    F. PLAY WITHOUT BALL   _____
    G. OVERALL   _____

REBOUNDING

    A. BLOCKING OUT   _____
    B. AGGRESSIVENESS   _____
    C. JUMPING ABILITY   _____
    D. TURN IN AIR   _____
    E. ABILITY TO OUTLET   _____
    F. MOVEMENT TO OFF.
       BOARDS   _____
    G. OVERALL   _____

PHYSICAL ABILITY

    A. WEIGHT   _____
    B. STRENGTH   _____
    C. JUMPING   _____
    D. SPEED/QUICKNESS   _____
    E. ENDURANCE   _____
    F. OVERALL   _____

ATTITUDE/PERSONALITY/COACHABILITY

    A. GENERAL ATTITUDE   _____
    B. WILLINGNESS TO
       WORK/SACRIFICE   _____
    C. TEAM SPIRIT   _____
    D. WILLINGNESS TO LEARN
       AND TAKE CORRECTIONS   _____
    E. LOVE FOR COACH, MATES,
       AND THE GAME   _____
    F. OVERALL   _____

FINAL COMMENTS

Coach's Signature:_____

This emphasizes the groin area. The player sits, opens his legs as far as comfortably possible. Legs should be straight, feet upright and relaxed at ankles. The player then leans forward AT THE HIPS as indicated. Hold for 20 seconds (Diagram 2.2 and 2.3).

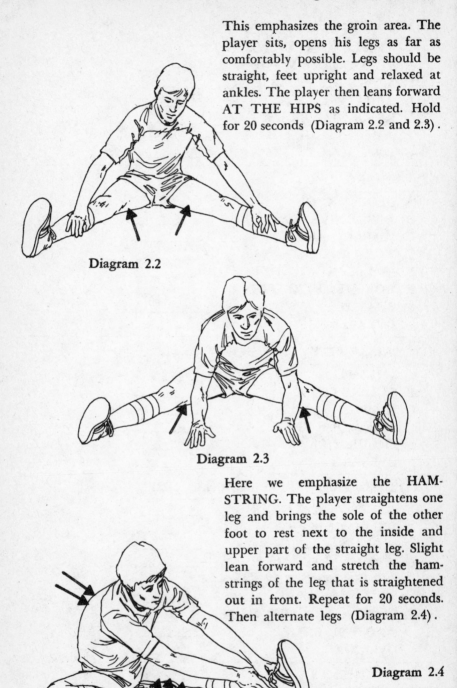

Diagram 2.2

Diagram 2.3

Here we emphasize the HAM-STRING. The player straightens one leg and brings the sole of the other foot to rest next to the inside and upper part of the straight leg. Slight lean forward and stretch the hamstrings of the leg that is straightened out in front. Repeat for 20 seconds. Then alternate legs (Diagram 2.4).

Diagram 2.4

Another groin exercise. Move the leg forward until the knee of the forward leg is directly over the ankle. Your other knee should be resting on the gym floor. Lean forward without changing the position of the knee on the gym floor or the forward foot. Do for 20 seconds. Then switch legs (Diagram 2.5).

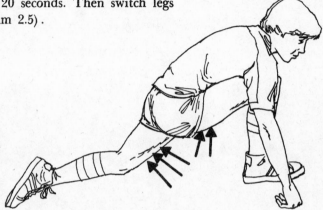

Diagram 2.5

In stretching the calf, player stands a little ways from the wall and leans on the wall with the forearms, head resting on the hands. Bend one leg and place the foot on the floor in front, leaving the other leg straight. The player should then slowly move the hips forward until he feels a stretch in the calf of the straight leg. Do not bounce. Hold for 20 seconds. Switch legs (Diagram 2.6A).

Diagram 2.6A

To stretch the soleus and Achilles' tendon, bend slightly the back knee, keeping the foot flat. This will give a much lower stretch which is also good for maintaining or regaining ankle flexibility. 20 seconds each leg (Diagram 2.6B).

Diagram 2.6B

Our captains lead in counting the twenty seconds in the form of 1000-1, 1000-2, and so on. After completing these, the players have two additional minutes to stretch on their own with whatever exercises they feel necessary.

We constantly emphasize to the players that stretching should be done slowly. There should be no bouncing or jerky movements. We don't want a strain or anything that causes pain. The key is to be relaxed. We don't do any stretch for longer than 20 seconds. And we try to increase the range ovver a long period. We stretch every day in practice at the beginning of our practice session. We encourage our players to do so over the summer before all workouts. And finally, our players do stretch in the locker room before taking the court on game nights. Several years ago, we actually came out on the court and stretched as a team, much like football teams do. But the cat-calls from the crowd put undue stress and embarrassment upon the players. So now we stretch in the locker room prior to the game.

Strength Training

Next is the weight training or strength portion of the program. Our players work on the Nautilus machine at one of the many clubs in and around the area, or they are free to come over to school where our weight room, which houses free weights and our Universal, is open all summer to any student. Some of our players even have sets of weights at home.

The basic OFF-SEASON workout program is this: on Mondays and Wednesdays the post man will work on his upper body; on Tuesdays and Thursdays the lower body. In each instance, we use the following formula to work with:

FIND MAXIMUM .. subtract 70 .. add 20 .. add 20 ..
subtract 10 .. subtract 20

$$\text{MAXIMUM} - (70) + (20) + (20) - (10) - (20)$$

The player does five reps with each weight and the last one is a "burn out"—as many as he can before stopping. He uses this formula in doing the following exercises (Diagrams 2.7, 2.8 and 2.9) :

NOTE—The diagrams (2.7 - 2.12) are all for use on the UNIVERSAL. The formula works best and quickest with this machine

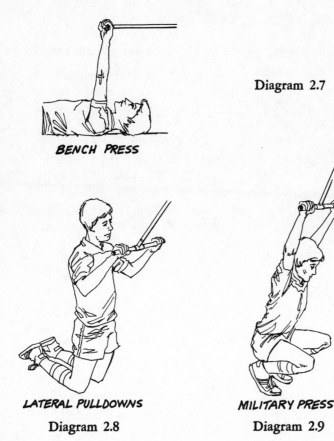

Diagram 2.7

BENCH PRESS

LATERAL PULLDOWNS

Diagram 2.8

MILITARY PRESS

Diagram 2.9

The player ends with workout with 5 minutes of rope jumping with a weighted vest or 2-3 minutes of jumping holding a brick in each hand.

On Tuesday and Thursday, the player will work on his lower body. Using the same formula [MAXIMUM — (70) + (20) + (20) — (10) — (20 — burn out] the player will do the following (Diagrams 2.10, 2.11 and 2.12):

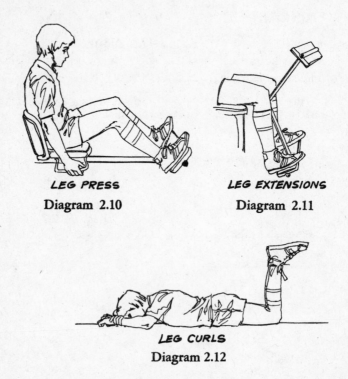

LEG PRESS
Diagram 2.10

LEG EXTENSIONS
Diagram 2.11

LEG CURLS
Diagram 2.12

HEEL RAISES—Stand upright. Place a (2 x 4) board under heels. Raise off the floor on toes and lift heels. Do three sets of 8, lowering the heel very slowly after raising it.

Again, we conclude with 5 minutes of rope jumping with a weighted vest or 2-3 minutes of jumping while holding a brick in each hand.

Running

Running is an integral part of strength buildup and agility. We therefore give the player an option of three running programs. We ask him to run a minimum three times a week and to note this in his letter to me.

Program "A"— Cross Country Running. This program involves 30 minutes of running or jogging anywhere. The player runs till fatigued, walks till rested, runs again, but stops after 30 minutes.

Program "B"—Lap Program. We use the football field for this. The player sprints 40 yards. Walks the next 10 yards. Sprints the next 40 yards. Runs backward around the goal post and end zone and repeats the same on the other side of the field.

After completing the field once, the player rests 30 seconds. He then repeats. We encourage our post men to try to start out by doing this 3-4 times and trying to increase it each time out by as much as he can (Diagram 2.13).

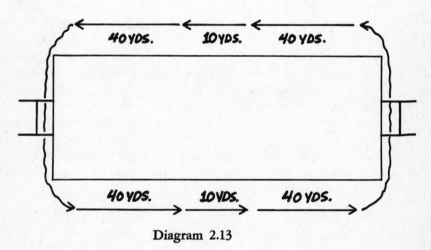

Diagram 2.13

Program "C"—Sprint Program. Run ten 40 yard sprints with a 15 second rest between each. Each sprint must be run as hard as one can. Time self if possible. Goal is to be between 5.0 and 5.9 for each one.

You might be wondering at this point how I arrived at the various formulas or programs and their goals. I wrote to over thirty colleges and universities around the country and asked for the programs that they use for their big men over the summer and during the pre-season. After going over their responses, I picked and chose, adopted and adapted, and came up with the combination that I employ. Obviously, I had to make adjustments for the youth and lack of strength on the part of the high school players.

As part of our off-season program, we ask our post man to shoot 300 shots per day and keep a record of them as best he can. We tell him to shoot any type of shot that he wants, but encourage him to shoot the power lay-up, the short hooks with both hands, and the turn-around jumper inside the lane and off the lane using the board.

We encourage him to play as much as possible. All literature that comes to us concerning summer camps is posted. We do not force or even encourage our players to go to camps. We have confidence in our program. Instead, we encourage him to use the programs that we give him. And, if he uses these programs faithfully and enthusiastically, HE WILL BECOME A BETTER PLAYER.

We do encourage participation in summer league programs. Though we do not demand it, when a player expresses an interest in playing, we will do our best to place him in such a league.

Finally, we encourage all players to take the weekend (Friday, Saturday, and Sunday) off from all types of basketball activities. No coach wishes to burn out his players before the season begins. We have had the youngster who tells us that he has too many other things to do over the summer and can't comply with any of our suggested activities. Some do tell us that they can get ready for the season when school begins. Our reaction to this very calm and unperturbed. We wish him good luck in his endeavors (many play summer baseball) and tell him that we'll see him in September. Our whole approach is very organized and business-like and programmed, YET VERY LOW-KEYED. It is an optional program and really a self-improvement program for THOSE WHO WANT IT.

PRE-SEASON

We define the pre-season as the time between the start of school and the official start of practice. We think that we have a unique philosophy and system as regards the pre-season. Coincidental with that, our first day of practice is just as unique.

From the time that school starts till the time official practice starts is six to eight weeks. During that time, many of our youngsters will be participating in other sports. This program is not for them. This program is for those who are not playing and will probably be up in the gym shooting or scrimmaging two or three times per week.

I don't like conditioning drills just for the sake of conditioning. When the bell rings for the official start of practice, the players want to GET AT IT. They want to start working on skill development, team offense, team defense. So I tell them that if they get themselves into some semblance of shape, we will get to the "fun" part of practice more quickly than ever. To be certain that they are in some "semblance of shape," I test our players on the first day of practice. We have done this for the last eight years and it has proved effective. Our players know that on the first official day of practice (November 1), they will be asked to do the following:

1. Run two miles.
2. Interval sprinting.
3. Perform a defensive slide for 20 seconds.
4. Rope jump for 1 minute.
5. Bench jump for 20 seconds.
6. Shoot layups.
7. Run our line touch drill.
8. Run our double line touch drill.

We also post, besides the various test, certain parameters—passing grades or various grade levels—that each player must meet in order to "pass" each test. Also each grade has a weighted value of from 1 to 5 points attached to it. This is done in order that we might measure each player against one another and determine who is in the best shape at each position—guard, forward, post men. See the example of the entire sheet—drill or test, with grades, and the weight that each carries with it. See page 30.

Each candidate for the team MUST "pass" each test and also accumulate a minimum of 30 total points when the entire series of tests is completed. Failure to pass a specific test or tests means that the athlete must repeat that particular test or tests before he is allowed to attend practice. Failure to accumulate a total of 30 points means that the athlete must repeat the entire series of tests even though he may not have failed a single test. (As you can see, it is possible to pass every test with a "1" and not make the final passing score of 30).

A brief explanation of each test is in order.

2 Mile Run. The purpose of this test is purely conditioning. We run on a track and are quite generous with the times. We are not trying to develop Olympic champions. We simply want our athletes to have run several times before taking this test so that they know they can do it.

Interval Sprinting. This, again, is pure conditioning. But is is more realistic as regards basketball because it emphasizes sprinting and, after a short recovery period, sprinting again. This is a taxing exercise and requires the individual to have done it several times prior to the test in order to condition himself for it. The scoring is rather subjective in this one, as the coach watches the players, times them, and then assigns point values ranging from 1 to 5 depending on their respective showing.

THE FIRST DAY OF BASKETBALL PRACTICE

"Get Yourself Physically Ready"

2-MILE RUN
under 11:45 ...... 5 pts
11:46 - 12:05 ...... 4 pts
12:06 - 12:30 ...... 3 pts
12:31 - 13:15 ...... 2 pts
13:16 - 14:00 ...... 1 pt
over 14:00 ...... FAILURE

INTERVAL SPRINTING
5 - 100 yd. sprints. Each boy must complete each sprint in 17 seconds with a minute time after the race to get back to the starting point. IF A BOY is in the process of walking back to starting line and the 1 min. interval elapses, he cannot start the next 100 yd. sprint until he reaches the starting line.

SUBJECTIVE SCORING: 5 - excellent 1 - very poor

ROPE JUMPS (1 min.)
over 175 .... 5 pts
161 - 174 .... 4 pts
150 - 160 .... 3 pts
140 - 149 .... 2 pts
130 - 139 .... 1 pt
under 130 ...... FAILURE

BENCH JUMPS (arms up-20 sec.)
35 .... 5 pts
32 - 34 .... 4 pts
28 - 31 .... 3 pts
23 - 27 .... 2 pts
17 - 22 .... 1 pt
under 17 .... FAILURE

DEFENSIVE SLIDE (arms up)
20 sec./20 ft.
over 16 touches .... 5 pts
15 .... 4 pts
13-14 .... 3 pts
11-12 .... 2 pts
10 .... 1 pt
under 10 .... FAILURE

TWO BALL LAY-UPS
(10 each side)
under 1:06 .... 5 pts
1:06 - 1:09 .... 4 pts
1:10 - 1:14 .... 3 pts
1:15 - 1:19 .... 2 pts
1:20 - 1:24 .... 1 pt
over 1:24 .... FAILURE

SINGLE LINE TOUCH
(arms up)
26 secs .... 5 pts
27-28 .... 4 pts
29 .... 3 pts
30 .... 2 pts
31 .... 1 pt
over 31 .... FAILURE

DOUBLE LINE TOUCH
(arms up)
under 60 secs ...... 5 pts
61 secs .... 4 pts
62 - 63 secs .... 3 pts
64 - 65 .... 2 pts
66 - 67 secs .... 1 pt
over 67 secs ...... FAILURE

FREE THROWS
Each player will shoot 15 free throws, receiving 1 pt for each one made.

NOTE * PLAYER MUST HAVE A CUMULATIVE SCORE OF AT LEAST "30" TO PASS AND NOT FAIL ANY SINGLE ACTIVITY.**

Rope Jumps. Though, as you will read later, we don't feel that jumping is the key to rebounding, we do feel that it important in co-ordination, agility, and the development of footquickness. This is why we incorporated it into the battery of tests. Most scores for this fall between the 161-174 range.

Bench Jumps. The bench employed is two feet high. Because of our philosophy on rebounding, this test is more difficult than it first appears. Our athletes must keep both arms above their head and jump on a "touch and go" principle. We do not allow the "gather step." When the athlete jumps over the bench he must go right back over again without a slight hesitation or a shuffling of his feet to catch his breath or regain his balance. The coaches watch very closely on this and force the player to repeat if he hedges on the purpose. Remember the arms must be up at all times.

Defensive Slide. We set this test up by placing a piece of tape on the floor and two other pieces of tape 10 feet on either side of the first one. See Diagram 2.14.

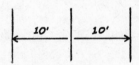

Diagram 2.14

The player's arms are once again above his head. He begins straddling the center line and on the whistle proceeds to slide in a defensive stance with the arms up and touch the outer edges of the outside lines as many times as he can in 20 seconds.

TWO BALL LAYUPS. The purpose of this drill is to condition the player to shoot the ball when fatigued and to take it up tough and strong to the basket. The test is set up in the following manner:

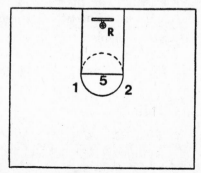

Diagram 2.15

Two basketballs are placed along the outer edges of the free throw line—one on each side. A ball "placer" stands next to each ball (this could be managers or players). These are designated by #1 and #2 in Diagram 2 - 15. A rebounder stands underneath the bucket out of bounds. The player taking the test stands at the center of the free throw line. The drill is designed so that the player must take 10 layups on the right and 10 layups from the left, using the specific hand on each side. He must alternate sides—right, left, right, left. He must do it in 1:24 seconds or he has failed the test. He need not worry about rebounding the shot—the rebounder does that and returns the ball to the ball placer who sets it in its proper spot.

The drill is a tough one, requiring good stamina, good quickness, and good layup shooting touch. The pressure mounts as the coach counts down the time. One miss and the player is practically finished. He must rebound a miss until it goes in. The coach must be certain that the players designated as the "ball placers" SET the ball down instead of rolling it, passing it, or bouncing it to the shooter. The very fact that the shooter must bend over, pick the ball up off the floor, and then go to the hoop is an important part of the drill. There is no way to pass this test without practicing it prior to the testing time. The player must determine the speed, the rhythm, and the pace at which he is to do this drill in order to be successful.

Single Line Touch Drill. All coaches run some variations of this. This is the drill where the player starts at the end line, touches the opposite end line and returns to the start, touches the free throw line and returns to the start, touches the 10 second line and returns to the start, and touches the free throw line at his end and returns to the start (Diagram 2.16).

The one stipulation that we place on our players in the running of our line touches is that his arms must be up above the shoulders—in other words, arms up, hands above the head while running. Our playing court is 90 feet long and hence our times are geared to that.

Double Line Touch Drill. The player runs the same drill as the single line touch but touches each line twice, instead of once.

Free Throws. After the completion of his double line touch test, the player picks up a basketball, goes over to an empty basket and shoot 15 feet throws without a practice toss. He reports his score out of 15 and calls it a day.

If the player has failed any one test, he cannot take it over on the testing day. He must make arrangements with the coaching staff to take it over on another day. I might add, that our staff is usually

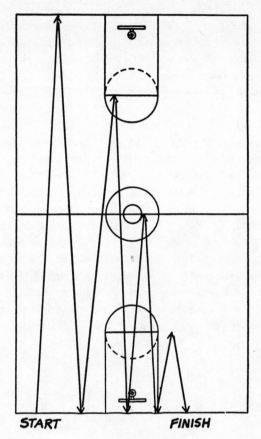

START   FINISH

Diagram 2.16

available at some odd times for make-up tests—7 a.m. on Saturday or Sunday morning. In some cases, because our staff is now tied up with practice, the player may have to wait two or three or four days before making up the test. Of course, he is not allowed to practice with the rest of the squad until he has made up the test.

We post the results of the tests the very next day. Our players are divided into back court and front court players—guards being designated as back court men, bigger people as front men. The winner—the player with the highest cumulative point total—in each division (front court, back court) is given a special award: steak dinner, tickets to a concert, tickets to a pro game, or the like.

The question inevitably arises as to what to do when a "star" player fails the tests or has not accumulated the required point totals. The answer is simple. MAKE HIM TAKE IT OVER AT YOUR

CONVENIENCE. TREAT HIM NO DIFFERENTLY FROM ANY-
ONE ELSE. Our philosophy is that if a youngster is not willing to
work on these prior to the official start of practice so that he can be
in some semblance of shape when we begin, then he is not going to
sacrifice for us or his teamates in the clutch during the season anyway.
And yes, we have had some players who, because of repeated failure to
pass one or another of the tests, ended by just giving up and quitting
the squad. Good riddance. They are not winners anyway.

So in summary, our pre-season work is really not mandatory. Each
player knows what is expected of him on that first official day of
practice. He is on his own to pre-test himself and see whether he
can pass the tests. We don't check on him during the pre-season. But
we do strictly enforce the rule that if you fail, you don't practice. Our
players are chomping at the bit to hit the hardwood come November.
And it is a blow to their ego to know that they cannot practice with
the team. Therefore, though not mandatory, it is a very common sight
to see our basketball players jumping rope, running two miles, sprinting
up and down the football field, doing the line touch drills, or jumping
over benches during the months of September and October as they
prepare for that FIRST DAY OF PRACTICE.

3

DRILLS TO DEVELOP
AGILITY AND REACTION

Since the multi-purpose area of the court is the key determinant in the outcome of a basketball game, it is of utmost importance to have a post player who can react well to given situations, who is co-ordinated, and who shows some agility. REACTION involves quick movement and shifting; CO-ORDINATION involves the bringing of different parts of the body into a working harmony; and AGILITY requires easy motion, with a minimum of strain.

Especially if you do want to put that tall, rather slow kid in the middle, do you need to emphasize in daily drills the development of these three qualities. Even your good athlete has to be drilled in various activities and situations that demand quick reaction, Co-ordination of the mind, hands, and feet, and easy, fluid motion.

The drills outlined here are designed for the pivot man. This is not to say that they cannot be used for other members of the squad. Their prime objectives are to develop REACTION, CO-ORDINA-TION, and AGILITY within the key or multi-purpose area.

JUMPING DRILLS

To be able to jump requires co-ordination and agility. You have already noticed the emphasis that we place on rope jumping. As mentioned before, we stress jumping—not because we believe it is the key to rebounding—but because we feel that jumping does help co-ordination and agility.

Continuous Jumping. We do a lot of continuous jumping drills to build endurance. The players simply jump, holding a basketball directly above their heads with both hands. They go off both feet and keep this up for 2-3-4-5 minute stretch. We have jumped continuously for up to 10 minutes. We often play music over the loudspeakers to take the player's minds off the monotony or we allow them to talk.

Jumping with Bricks. In order to increase arm strength, we have our post man jump with a brick in each hand. This is much more difficult than simply holding the basketball. The amount of time here has to be cut drastically. Even two minutes is very taxing.

Jumping Sequence. Our jumping sequence is a series of jumps—twenty-five of each. It only takes minutes to perform. (1) The player jumps 25 times off both feet, arms extended up in the air. We allow a slight rotation of the hands as the shoulders lower to help propel the body upward. (2) The player next jumps 25 times off the right foot. (3) He then goes 25 times off the left foot. (4) Next is 25 jumps where the player brings his knees up as close as possible to his chest. (5) Then 25 jumps where the player kicks his heels near to his buttocks behind him. (6) 25 spread eagle jumps, whereby the player jumps, spreads his legs out as far as possible while in mid air and touches the fingers of his hands to his toes. The legs are greatly strengthened by these jumps, endurance is built up, and co-ordination and agility are both increased.

Diagonal Rope Jump. This drill adds a degree of difficulty to each jump. Simply secure a rope at one end near ground level. Tie the rope at the other end in such a manner that it gets higher as it gets closer to the end. In other words, the post man must jump over the rope on a touch and go principle and try to get as far along up the rope as possible. We do this for 20 seconds.

Second Effort Drill. This drill involves determining the height of the post man's jump and marking that spot either on the backboard or the rim with a small piece of colored tape. The player stands under the board and goes up to touch that spot as many times as he can before he misses it. He must use the touch and go principle—no stagger or gather step. He counts each touch when he hits his spot. You'd be surprised how this helps to increase the vertical jump as well as develop a great second, third and fourth effort in the youngster.

Board-Reaction Drill. This drill has the player touching his spot on the board, but now he runs to the free throw line and touches that with his hand between every jump. He is working against the clock and his own personal goals for touching his spot.

Knock-Knock Drill. This drill emphasizes co-ordination and suspension of the body in mid-air. The player starts from the free throw line, sprints toward the hoop, jumps, and touches his hand on the rim NOT ONCE but twice. To do this, he must hang in the air. If a player can hit the rim three times or more before landing back on the floor, you have a well co-ordinated individual.

Hang Time Drill. To help co-ordination and agility, we have the player start from the top of the key and sprint toward the hoop. We then have him leave the floor at the circle (see Diagram 3.1 "x" marks the spot), extend his arm, hang in the air and try to touch the rim.

Next, he leaves the floor at the free throw line, thrusts his body toward the rim, and tries to hit the rim before landing on the floor.

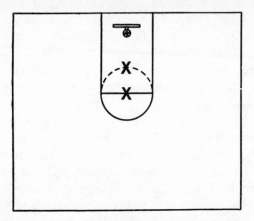

Diagram 3.1

All of our jumping drills are designed to help leg, arm, and body co-ordination and agility in our post man. We use one or two of these daily.

REACTION DRILLS

Too often coaches simply want to teach their post men how to shoot and what moves to make inside. We feel that before this can be done we must develop good reaction in our player. Good reaction implies quick, sure hands and legs that move quickly and under control at all times. Good hands are essential to the post man: he must catch the poorly thrown pass, pick up loose balls on the floor, rebound, outlet, get a hand up in the face of a shooter, stop dribble penetration. We also demand that our post man run down court at all times *under control.* We want him to jump under control, not wildly where he picks up unnecessary fouls. We want him to post up well, using his legs and body. Finally, he must be able to bend the knees, stay down, and play good positional post defense.

Our reaction drills are designed to help increase agility, co-ordination, and quickness of the post players. Most of the drills have secondary purposes, also. Drills should be multi-faceted and multi-functional to save time. Basketball is a game of reaction, and anything that we as coaches can do to improve an individual's reaction will help that person become a better player and help our team become a better team.

Pivoting. This is one fundamental that needs much work and is often taken for granted. A player, especially the post man, must know how to pivot. He uses the pivot to get open inside, to protect the ball when thrown inside, and to make his move to the basket. The pivot is fundamental to co-ordination and is good test of agility. To see the player come to a jump stop, maintain good body balance, pivot in good basketball position, and remain in body balance is a sure sign that the post man is on his way to developing.

The way that we teach the pivot is quite basic. We line the player up at the 10 second line and have him run to the free throw line where he comes to a jump stop—both feet parallel, knees flexed, hands out in front of him, palms facing the baseline. On the whistle, the player executes a reverse pivot off the right foot. We check to make certain that on the pivot he maintains body balance, that he does not raise from the bent or flexed knee position, and that his hands and head remain relatively still, almost in the exact same place they were at the start of the pivot. Failure to accomplish any of these means that the player has lost some body balance in the process of the pivot.

After the pivot has been executed, we check again to make certain that the knees are flexed, feet are parallel, and hands and arms in their proper position. We emphasize that there should be a whip-like action of the non-pivot leg as it pulls around on the pivot. We tell our post man that he must be physical and not be afraid of contact.

We alternate pivot feet and repeat the process again. We use both the front pivot and rear pivot. As the player improves, we emphasize reaction to the whistle and more quickness in the pivot.

Once we are satisfied with the skeleton form of the pivot, we add a defensive player. Now we stress that the offensive player must step into the defender, make contact, and with the hips lowered and knees bent, execute a reverse pivot by thrusting the non-pivot leg via a whip-like action around and across the defender. The defense is told to be relatively passive in this phase of the drill.

The third phase of the sequence adds a man at the 10 second line with a basketball. The offensive player (#1) and the defender (#2) line up as shown in Diagram 3.2. Notice the position of #3 with the basketball. The offensive player moves toward the free throw line towards the defense. As he approaches, the offensive man executes a reverse pivot, as the defense tries to fight around. Timing is now essential as player #3 passes the basketball to #1 as he completes his pivot. We stress that the ball should be thrown about one count prior to the pivot. It is almost like a timing pattern along the sideline in football.

There are many other variations that we use off this set. More in a later chapter.

Cut and Go Drill. The floor is marked with tape as indicated in Diagram 3.3. The idea of the drill is for the player to hit the "X" with the outside foot, plant it firmly and push off in a quick change of direction. Sounds, easy! Well, it isn't. On each taped X the player must plant the outside foot and push off. It involves concentration and co-ordination. We are not interested in speed. Timing is essential and the maintenance of foot co-ordination is a positive corollary to the drill.

Body Obstacle Race. This activity is designed to increase foot agility, co-ordination, and quickness in reaction. It is also a competitive activity and the players have a lot of fun with it. The squad is divided into two teams with an equal number of players on each squad. The players lie prone on their backs in a straight line as indicated in Diagram 3.4.

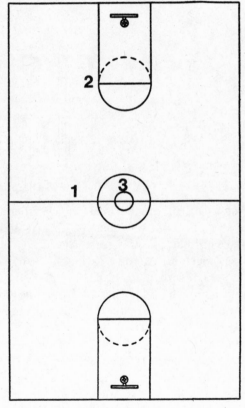

Diagram 3.2

When the drill is run for the first time, the players should be 5-6 feet apart. The relay race begins with the player first in line running and jumping over the players who lie prone on their backs. As he reaches the last player he turns around and, still jumping over his prone teammates, returns to his original position. When he lands at his original position, he flops to the floor on his back and yells "GO" which is the key for the next player in line to go and repeat the same procedure. When that player has gone down and back and returned to his original starting spot, he hits the floor and yells "GO" which is the key for the next player to begin. This procedure continues until all players have run the relay and a winner is determined.

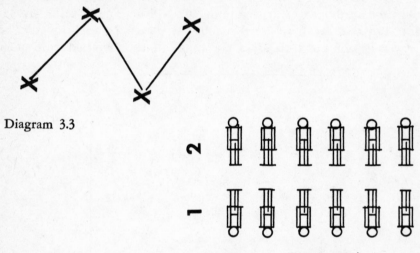

Diagram 3.3

Diagram 3.4

Variations of this drill can be made by lengthening the distance between the bodies on the floor—thus making it more difficult for the timing and co-ordination. Also, one can bring the players lying on the floor closer together. Another variation is to make the players jump over each person with a PULL-UP JUMP—jump off both feet. And finally, you can run the relay backward over the prone players. All of these are fun and serve to increase the foot co-ordination and agility of team members.

Basketball Pickup. The set-up of this drill is shown in Diagram 3.5. Player #1 is holding a basketball. Player #2 is positioned 6-8 feet in front of #1. The player with the ball rolls it to the left of #2 so that #2 has to slide about 8-10 feet in order to pick it up. Player #2 then returns the ball to #1 and begins to slide laterally in the opposite direction. #1 proceeds to roll the ball to his right about 8-10 feet away. We repeat this movement for 20 seconds.

When the players have become acquainted with the drill, we have two basketballs and make it a TWO BALL PICKUP. Not only must the man sliding and picking up the ball concentrate and work hard, but now the man rolling the ball must be quick. As he rolls one ball in one direction, another ball is returning from the other. If the drill is run properly, #1 should be rolling a ball to one side, and just at about the time he has released the rolled ball, another ball should be coming towards him on a pass from #2. The drill combines concentration with good hand reaction on the part of the passer and obvious foot reaction on the part of the man picking up the basketballs.

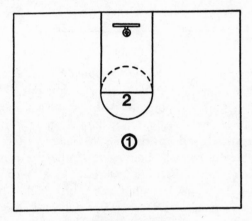

Diagram 3.5

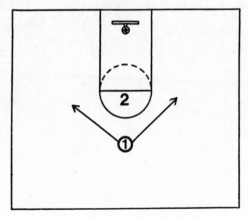

Diagram 3.6

Blind Catch. We expect our post man to be able to catch any pass that comes his way, whether it be a good pass or a bad one. We also expect our post man to develop good peripheral vision. To help achieve these goals, the coach (X) lines up as shown in Diagram 3.7. The post player (#5) stands at the middle post with his back to the coach.

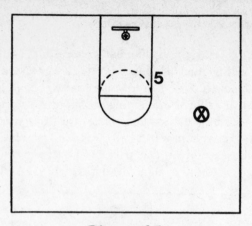

Diagram 3.7

On the verbal signal of "NOW" shouted by the coach, the player executes a quick jump-turn. The coach, meanwhile, has passed the ball toward the post man—a bounce pass, chest pass, lob, or whatever. The post man must find the ball, catch it cleanly, and power to the basket. For variation, and to· develop a sense of locating the ball quickly, we will roll the ball, bounce it at the player's feet, or hurl it straight up in the area about 30 feet to confuse the player and force him into quicker reactions. Another variation of the drill is to pass the ball first and then shout "NOW"—thus demanding an even quicker jump-turn pivot from the post man. If he doesn't turn quickly and get those arms and hands ready to catch the ball, it will get him first.

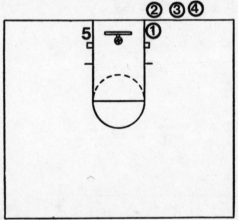

Diagram 3.8

React and Block. This drill is designed to increase the post man's foot and hand reaction while helping his skills in shot blocking. It also helps to teach "drawing the charge." The drill is set up as shown in Diagram 3.8. #5 is the post man, while #1 is holding a basketball. Other squad members line up out of bounds, each holding a ball, awaiting their turn. The drill begins when player #1 rolls his basketball toward the free throw line oppposite, at the juncture where it meets the circle. This is shown is diagram 3.9 with an X.

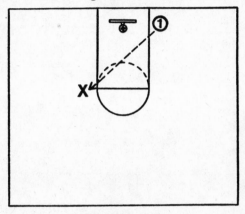

Diagram 3.9

As soon as the ball begins to roll on the floor, #1 goes chasing after it. The rolled basketball MUST hit the free throw line at the point X where it meets the circle as shown in DIAGRAM 3.9. As soon as #1 has rolled the ball on the floor, the post man slides across the lane to the BOX (first free throw marking), touches it with his hand or foot and then slides up the lane to touch the second free throw lane mark with his hand or foot. In the meantime, #1 has hustled over to pick up the basketball that he has rolled and now drives in for a layup. The post man, after touching his marks, now reacts to try to either block #1's shot or get in front of him for the charge or to harass him in any way so that he misses the shot. Diagram 3.10 shows the path of both players—#1 and #5 (the post man).

This is an excellent drill and serves many purposes. Besides the obvious reaction on the post man's part, conditioning is a necessary result as we usually make the post man go through the entire team before he retires from the drill.

We vary the drill by allowing #1 to shoot the jumper from the free throw line extended, should he choose to do so. This forces our post man to react now by getting an arm and hand up in the face of the shooter.

A third variation is to allow the second man in line (#2) to step out to the box and thereby create a 2-on-1 situation. The end of the drill is shown in Diagram 3.11. #1 has rolled his basketball, gone ofter it, and picked it up. #5 has completed his slide across the lane and is now in the process of moving toward the driving #1. Meanwhile #2 has stepped out to the BOX and created a 2 on 1 situation.

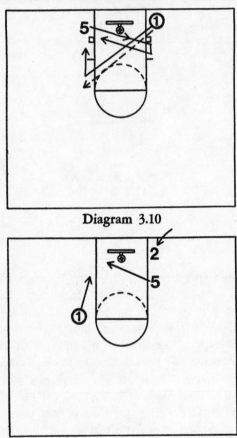

Diagram 3.10

Diagram 3.11

Shot Blocker. Quick hand/leg reaction on the part of the post man is the purpose of this drill. The set-up is shown in Diagram 3.12. #4 has the basketball. #5 is our post man in a defensive position facing offensive players #1, #2, and #3. With his back to the man out of bounds. post man #5 must react to a pass in bounds to any one of the three offensive players. The offensive players are instructed, upon receiving the pass, to power towards the basket. The post man must react and distract the shooter or block his shot. Contact results, but it is fun. #5 must really be quick and use good vision in order to stop a sure layup.

One-on-One Mirror Drill. The post man lines up eyeball to eyeball with another player. The post man gets into a defensive position and places his nose as close to his teammate's chest as possible. The other player moves laterally: right-left, right-left. The post man reacts and moves with him, working hard, but always keeping that forehead and nose as close to the chest of his teammate as possible.

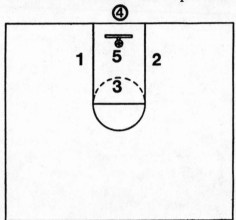

Diagram 3.12

Low Post Defensive Reaction Drill. Reaction and proper defensive post positioning are the goals of this drill. The alignment of players is shown in Diagram 3.13 X5 is our defensive post man and he must guard #4 and #6 who must remain stationary on the blocks, #2, #3, and #1 are the passers who try to get in into #4 and #6. The ball is started with #2.

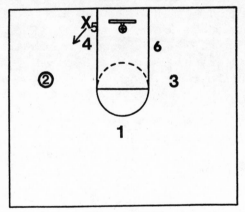

Diagram 3.13

We allow our post man to position himself correctly on the baseline side of #4 with an arm extended into the passing lane. No one man moves or cuts in this drill except the defensive post man. The ball is rotated around the perimeter as Number #1, 2, and 3 try to jam the ball inside to either of the low post men. When #4 or #6 gets the ball, they shoot it and battle for a missed shot off the boards. The feed inside can be made from the wing area or from the point by #1.

The drill accomplishes a lot. It forces the defensive post man to react quickly and play good positional defense. We encourage him to get on the baseline side when the ball is in the possession of #2 or #3. We want him on the high side, between his man and the ball when the ball is out front in possession of #1. The drill is also useful for the other players. #4 and #6 are taught to post up in proper position. And the three perimeter players work on their passing as they try to get the ball inside to the multi-purpose area.

Combo Shooting Drill. Although more will be said about offensive moves and special shooting drills for the post man in later chapters, there is one shooting drill that we run daily that I feel comes under the heading of REACTION AND AGILITY. Our combo shooting drill emphasizes timing, quickness, and agility. It is a simple drill that involves two simple concepts: (1) don't allow the ball to hit the floor; (2) use proper footwork to achieve timing.

The post man starts the drill with a right-handed layup, catches the ball from the net and shoots a left-handed layup. After retrieving the ball from the net again, he takes a big stride back on the right side and shoots a short right-handed hook. Reacting back to the goal, he catches the ball as it goes through the net, takes a big stride towards the left side of the goal with his right foot, pushes off the right foot, and shoots a short left-handed hook. Then he catches the ball as it passes through the net, steps back toward the right side of the goal with his back to the baseline, and pushes off his right foot, as he shoots a left-handed buttonhook from the right side. He does the same on the left side, shooting a right-handed button-hook.

We have our post men repeat this drill twice, shooting a total of 12 shots in all. If the ball hits the floor, if a shot is missed, if the individual's timing and footwork is off, if he takes steps, he must do the entire sequence over again. It's not as easy as it might sound. Making twelve shots in a row, without the ball touching the floor, plus using proper footwork and timing is no small task.

These are just some of the drills that we use to increase co-ordination and agility in our players. Although we classify these drills under jumping and reaction, they serve to develop our post man into the multi-purpose type of player that we want him to be.

4

POST PLAY:
GAINING POSSESSION

In talking, working, dealing with the post man, it is important that both player and coach realize several important points.

PATIENCE is the key word in dealing with the post man. It takes a lot of time and effort for dividends to pay off, especially if your post man is extremely big. Both coach and player should not expect too much too soon. Both have to think positively. Both must have confidence in each other. It is important to establish this relationship. You, as coach, must come up with drills *early* in your practice sessions so that the player can become enthusiastic and develop confidence in himself and his coach. Nothing makes one work harder than success. Drills that are virtually impossible to accomplish are useless and futile. The post player must see and feel progress.

The post man must know that he is the focal point of the offense. When he gets the ball, he is the most important man on the court. He has to know the offense thoroughly. He has to be able to read defenses. He has to learn to be unselfish. He must know that the players will gladly give him the ball if they will get it back if nothing is there at the pivot.

The post man must be intelligent enough to recognize where or how the defense is playing him. On offense, the post man does not make up his mind on what move to use until he gets the ball. He lets the defense determine his method of receiving the ball and what he'll do after he gains possession of it.

The defense can only be playing one of the three ways: front, side, or directly behind. When the defender is behind, it is certain death and a sure score for us. We'll talk more about this as we proceed.

POSITIONING

As the ball is being brought upcourt, the post man should line up on the high side of the BOX (rectangle along foul lane). The post man should be FACING INTO THE LANE. Just this simple maneuver (facing the lane) causes many problems for the defender. A defensive man is simply not accustomed to see the man he is guarding squarely facing him and staring him in the eye. In such a position, the defensive post man usually feels mighty foolish playing in front of the offensive man.

As the ball is brought to the wing area of the court (free throw line extended), the post man's first step should be toward the baseline to drive his man down. Then he pivots into the defender to seal him off. The pivot must be executed properly—knees flexed, hips lowered, arm up with elbows out, taking up a lot of space on the court.

In order to perfect this move, TIMING between the guard-forward- and post man is essential. You must work on this daily, beginning without a defense. Diagram 4.1 shows the guard dribbling up court across the 10-second line, while the forward begins his move to get open. The post man (C), facing the lane, eyes the guard and, as the forward pops out to receive the ball, initiates his pivot move into the defensive center (in this case, against a "skeleton" center).

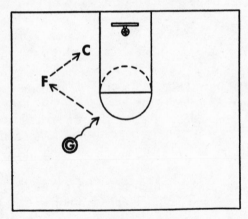

Diagram 4.1

The next phase of the drill is to add a defensive man on the offensive guard. This pressure on the guard will disturb the timing and force new adjustments by the forward and center.

Next add a second defender—one on the forward. And finally, add a third defender, one on the post man. When the defender is put on the post man, begin by making the defender play directly behind. Next allow him to play on the side—first the baseline side, then the high side. It is now that we make adjustments in our post positioning.

Generally speaking, each team will establish a certain pattern or trend on how to guard the post man. Usually this is based on the size match-up and scouting reports on the other players. But usually after two or three times downcourt, the coach can determine the trend. In fact, one of the first things any coach should look for from the bench is HOW THE OPPONENTS ARE DEFENSING THE PIVOT MAN. This determination is crucial in order for you to have offensive success in the ball game. It is one of the first things that the successful coach looks for as he observes the beginning of each game. An intelligent post player determines this, too, and should be able to verbalize this to the coach during an early time out. If your post man can come over to the bench and say confidently and correctly that they are "fronting me when I'm low and siding me on the baseline side when high" or "they are playing directly behind me at all times" or the like, you know you have an intelligent post player. If you have a post player who can read defenses like this, you are well on your way to developing a great pivot man.

When the ball is thrown to the forward at a wing position below the free throw line and the defensive post man is playing on the low side (baseline side), the post man should line up on the next posses-sion on the LOW SIDE OF THE BOX (see Diagram 4.2). If the defensive man is playing on the high side of the post, not the baseline side, the post man should move up the lane to straddle the second free throw mark, BUT he should stay on the lane.

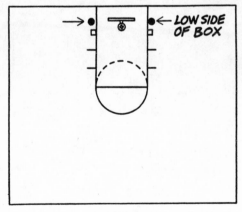

Diagram 4.2

If the defensive man is directly behind, get to the HIGH SIDE OF THE BOX. And if the defensive man is fronting (completely in front) of the post man, he should slide up the lane to the third free throw mark and move one half or one step off the lane.

More will be said later about the pass and the type of shot to be used, but in brief, if the defensive man is playing on the high side, the post man should expect a bounce pass or overhead pass and be thinking "POWER LAYUP." If the defender is on the LOW SIDE, he should be expecting a bounce, overhead or halo pass (one thrown between the head and outstretched arm of the defender—a quick wrist snap pass through the so-called "halo") and be thinking "HOOK IN MIDDLE." If the defender is BEHIND, a bounce, overhead, or halo pass should be expected and a quick pivot jumper or one-dribble-drive move should be used. If the defender is FRONTING, the post man should expect a lob pass from the forward at the strong wing, from the guard at the point as the post man swings into the lane (see Diagram 4.3) or from a weak forward who has flashed across high (see Diagram 4.4). The shot in all three cases will be a baby jumper or power layup. More will be developed on these techniques in a later chapter.

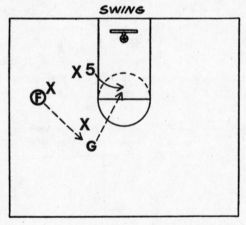

Diagram 4.3

At times, a team will try to change their manner of playing the post man on each and every possession. If this occurs and the defensive post man is constantly moving and sliding and running around with no definite pattern, he is easier to burn, provided that everyone on the team—guards and forwards—can recognize the defense. The defender can only play one way, on a given possession when the play is at a given position on the floor. It is of utmost importance that the coach explain and teach all of the post defensive recognition moves to each player on the squad. Remember, the post man is the focal point of your team and the hub of your offense. Every player must look to him and know what he is thinking and doing.

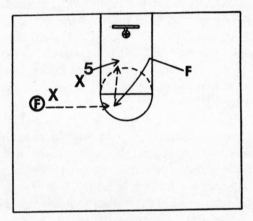

Diagram 4.4

THE TARGET

The first thing to teach the post man, after he learns to read defenses and how to combat them, is to "WANT THE BALL." He will never get the basketball unless he presents a *good target* to the passer. The hand and the arm farthest away from the defense is raised high in the air. If a player doesn't raise his arm, he will never get a pass. This rule is emphasized to the other players on the squad. Even though a bounce pass is the obvious pass to be made inside, the signal—the upraised arm and hand—must be given. This signal is the cue to the passer that the post man has positioned himself properly and now "WANTS THE BALL" and can GET IT IF THROWN CORRECTLY. This is crucial, because there may be times when the post man feels that he doesn't want the ball because he is not properly positioned or open. Then, no hand is put up.

The non-target hand or arm is to be positioned in one of two manners. The back of the hand is under the chin with palm open—elbow jutting out beyond the plane of the body. This will eliminate many pushing-off fouls and yet it does ward off the defender. The elbow jutting out is particularly effective against the defender who is playing on the side. Having an elbow in the chest is not very comfortable for the defense. When a team has a good-sized, well-proportioned post man, this method is an excellent one. Or when a team has a size advantage or mismatch in the post, this method of using the off-arm is very effective.

The second method of employing the non-target hand and arm is used by a smaller post man against a bigger defender. Since the smaller post man battling a larger defender must take up a lot of space, encourage him to spread out with good leg and knees position, wide base, target hand-arm raised up, and non-target hand extended outward directly parallel to the floor. If the referees begin to call an offensive foul on this move, it is obvious that the maneuver must be changed to the first one described.

The first method of using the non-target hand—that of placing the off-hand under the chin with the elbow protruding out into the defender —is also especially effective against the defender who is denying the post man the ball by fronting. The lob pass over the top of the defense is a very effective pass. When the pass is nullified, it is usually done so by an offensive pushing foul called against the post man. The first method of using the non-shooting hand/arm really prevents or minimizes the offensive push-off foul. Rarely will the officials call such a foul on the over-the-top pass if they don't see that hand in a pushing position with the palms facing the back of the defender.

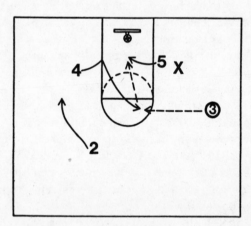

Diagram 4.5

Though more will be said later about the moves to combat the defensive front on the post, it is important to realize that the over-the-top pass is a difficult one to execute. With players so adept and willing to take the charge nowadays, weak side defensive men really cut this move off. It is often safer and more effective to bring the weak-side forward across, flare the point guard wide, and go to the weak forward who hits the post rolling to the basket. See Diagram 4.5. The post man (#5), using a reverse pivot, pins his defender on his hip, properly uses his off-arm, and rolls to the basket for a pass by the forward (#3).

THE PASS

"Anticipation" and "expectation" are two words that are important to a basketball player and to a basketball team. Each player on the team must be able to "anticipate" the opponent's moves and "expect" his own teammates to do certain things in certain situations. These are taught through concentrated efforts in practice as players read the defense and observe their teammates reaction to specific situations.

The post player must know his own players and their passing abilities. The post player, along with every player on the court, must know the type of pass to be used in a given situation. The post man can better handle a pass if he expects it to be of a certain type.

Passing skills are among the poorest of all skills that a basketball player possesses. Players begin early in their careers dribbling and shooting. But rarely do youngsters work on passing skills. A coach who emphasizes in daily practice various passing skills and drills is a coach who is or will be a winner.

The technique of passing is usually taught with emphasis on proper form—step towards the passer, knees flexed, release of the ball with thumb down, palms out. There is nothing wrong with teaching this method and form. But with players nowadays being so quick and so talented, with the talent level being very even in most cases at both the high school and collegiate level, it is often difficult to use proper form and raditional passes in game situations. The coach has to be more concerned with the pass "just getting there" than with proper form. The basic technique of passing—the basic axiom of form— might best be summed up in this manner: PASS AWAY FROM THE DEFENSE. Don't be concerned about spin on the ball and the form of the passer. Use the pass that will best get the ball to the offensive receiver—away from the defense.

The best places on the floor for the post man to be fed are from the free throw line extended or from the top of the key. The most difficult spot for the post man to be fed is the baseline. These concepts must be pointed out to all players. They must understand the game in order to play it well.

You should also emphasize to your players that they recognize when to pass and when not to pass. If the defender guarding the man with the ball is off him, then no pass is to be made. The man with the ball must re-adjust his position by putting the ball on the floor, thus making the defender guard him more tightly. Only when the man with the ball is tightly guarded is he in what can be labelled the "passing position." Young players tend to make the mistake of not knowing when to pass or when to shoot or when to drive. Reading the defense and recognizing when you are closely guarded is the key to passing the ball successfully. It is very difficult to pass the ball when the defender is in a sag position or off the man with the ball by two feet.

The basic pass into the post man is the bounce pass. Most defensive post men cannot get down quickly enough or low enough to get this particular pass. So, encourage post men to expect the bounce pass. Work on guard-forward-post timing using the bounce pass. Encourage perimeter players to master this pass.

As mentioned earlier, if the post man is being fronted, expect a lob pass. If sided, on the baseline side, expect the bounce pass, halo pass, or overhead flip pass. If sided on the high side, expect a bounce or overhead pass. If the defense is directly behind, expect the bounce pass.

These are the basic rules. Obviously, the defensive man guarding the passer might make him adjust. But, as a coach, you must work hard with your perimeter people and explain to them the same concepts that you relate to your post man.

CATCHING THE PASS

The post man is in proper position, giving the proper target with the target arm, placing the non-target arm in such a position so as not to draw the offensive foul and yet in a position to ward off the defender, recognizing the defense. The pass is on its way. All the post man has to do is CATCH the basketball and it is a cinch two points. Sounds simple! Well, many players have done all the items mentioned above but failed to catch the ball because they have not concentrated on this phase of the game. The coach has not thought it important enough to work on CATCHING in practice.

In catching the ball, the body should lean against the defender, using the hips and thighs to keep the defender away. Whenever possible, both hands should receive the pass—WITH THE PALMS OF THE HANDS FACING THE BALL. Never have the palms facing each other. This is grabbing the ball, not catching it. If a player can

catch the ball with one arm, that would be great. Don't encourage
this, but do work on it during practice. When the ball hits the post
man's target hand which has been raised in the air, teach him to balance
the ball on his wrist, cupping the fingers and palm over the ball. He
then brings the other hand over the ball in the chest area to protect it.
A dangerous way to catch the ball .... YES! It is better to catch it with
both hands, but if the coach hasn't worked on catching with one hand,
the post man cannot be expected to do it in game situations.

Like any other receiver, when sided or played directly from the rear,
the post man should come to the pass WITHOUT giving up a lot of
court position. When fronted, follow the rules outlined earlier and hold
ground while the pass is in the air. Above all, NEVER run away from
the ball. Don't go before the pass has arrived in your hand.

Once the pass has been received, it must be brought immediately
into the chest area and held right next to the chest with the elbows protruding outward. The head should be thrust quickly toward the baseline,
chin upon shoulder. These two maneuvers—the chesting of the ball and
the turning of the head immediately towards the baseline—are the
preliminary steps to the offensive move that will follow.

Combination drills used to teach post positioning, catching and
passing are many. Some of the better ones include these:

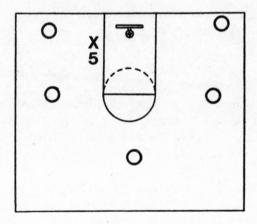

Diagram 4.6

Catch and Slide Drill. Players position themselves around the
perimeter as indicated in Diagram 4.6. The post man must slide and
move—not leaving the multi-purpose area—until he has received a pass
from each one of the five perimeter people. Once he has received a

pass from each player, then he can make a move to the basket. The defender battles and defends him as best he can. If the defense gets a hand on two passes, then he changes position with the offensive man. He goes to offense, while the offensive man goes to defense.

Blind Catch Drill. This drill is designed to get the post man into the habit of (1) finding the ball when it is in the air; (2) handling a pass that is poorly thrown; (3) making something good out of a bad situation. A coach is the passer in this drill, since a bad pass has to be made. Never allow players to make bad passes even in practice drill.

The set-up is as shown in Diagram 4.7.

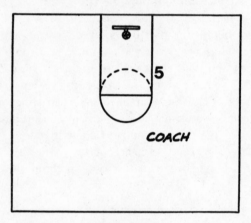

Diagram 4.7

The post man (#5) is facing the basket just as if he were set up prior to the ball being brought across court. The coach yells "NOW"— the post player executes a quick reverse pivot spin and sights the ball. The coach throws a deliberate poor pass—either at the post man's feet, or three or four feet to the side, or a bad lob. The post man has to find the ball and move to the basket. As a secondary part of the drill, add a defensive man on the post player.

Double Team Post Drill. This drill is designed for the post man to learn how to catch the ball in a crowd, then how to protect the ball, and finally how to dish it off to an open man. The setup of the drill is shown in Diagram 4.8.

Two defenders are assigned to the post man (#5). No defense is put on the other three offensive men. The ball must be thrown into the post man in the multi-purpose area before any shot is taken. Once the post man receives the ball, he is to dish it off to one of the perimeter players who move to open shooting slots. After the post man has mastered these techniques fairly well, put a defender on each perimeter player and play four offensive men against 5 defenders, with the post man still having two defenders on him. In this particular phase of the drill, inevitably another defender sags on the post man after he gets the ball, making three men on the pivot. The post man then has to find the open man. Encourage the perimeter players to sag and triple team the post when he gets the ball.

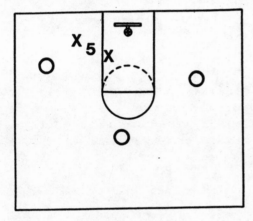

Diagram 4.8

5

POST PLAY: OFFENSE AFTER THE RECEPTION

Once the ball has been properly received in the multi-purpose area at the low post or mid post, the post man need only master three basic shots to be effective. These are: the power layup, the short hook, the turn-around jumper. In preparation and anticipation for these shots, it is important to have a teaching mechanism that makes the post man feel comfortable in shooting all of these.

THE MOVES AND THE SHOT

In practicing the power layup, timing, concentration, and body control are essential. The post man must work daily on this shot because it is his bread-and-butter shot. One minute working on powers from the right side and one minute working on them from the left side per day is the minimum amount of work needed.

Power Layup. In teaching the power layup, make certain that the post man jumps off both feet and, while protecting the ball, lunges to the basket—literally, "hurls his body" at the hoop. The coach should position himself on the rectangle along the lane *opposite* the side his player is shooting. Using the phrase "I want to see your back" makes the offensive player realize the importance of using the body to protect the ball, keeping his backside between the defender and the ball.

Variations of the drill can make the post man alternate right and left-handed power layups. After the coach feels confident that the player is taking the ball up tough inside and protecting it properly, a defensive man can be added. He tries to block the shot. Both players start at the low post position with the defender manning the inside position nearest the basket.

One of the most important components of shooting is concentration. In order to try to break the layup shooter's concentration, put a player with a hand fight-back dummy (type used by football players) and have him gently harass or nudge the shooter as he goes up for the power shot.

This maneuver at first tends to break the shooter's concentration. But ultimately he gets used to it and the physical contact that accompanies the drill.

After mastering the power move from a stand, it is essential that the post man be able to execute the move breaking to the ball and receiving a pass. The coach or passer should get in the right corner or the area below the foul line at a wing position. The post man should station himself opposite, on the left side of the lane and in a low post position. As the post man breaks to the ball, he should receive the pass in the proper manner as described in the previous chapter. As he catches the pass, it is important to land on both feet so that either can be declared the pivot foot. Without sliding either foot, the post man then thrusts his head over the left shoulder—shoulder closest to the baseline. When he sees no one DIRECTLY in his path, the post man should step toward the hoop with his left foot, dribble the ball with a hard, pounding motion, and execute a side step hop that will get him close to the basket. As he catches the ball off the dribble, he lands on both feet simultaneously again, with his back towards the middle of the lane. Without fully extending his knees, the post man should fake upward with the head, shoulders, arms, and ball—though the ball fake should not lift the ball above the head. Then propelling himself off both feet, he lunges into the basket and powers the ball off the backboard.

Short Hook Shot. In preparing the post man for the short hook shot, it is important for him to master and understand the basic theory of shooting that shot. In shooting the right-handed hook, the body is positioned in this manner: back to the basket with knees slightly bent. The head should turn left to pick up the target, while the post man pivots on and springs from his left foot. The left shoulder turns and points toward the target, while the right leg is raised to a position under the buttocks where the thigh is parallel to the floor.

The position of the basketball is as follows: the ball starts at waist level. It is placed in line of flight by fully extending the right arm with wrist action delivering the ball. The left arm folds and collapses and is used as a protective device against the defense. The index finger points to the basket and is the last to touch the ball. The ball is shot over the front rim from the front or immediate side. The ball is shot off the backboard when shooting 30 to 45 degree angle from the baseline. See Diagram 5.1.

An important coaching point deals with the "plant foot"—the push-off foot. The "plant" or push-off foot should be parallel to the backboard —toes pointed toward the sideline. The hook shot has to be mastered with both right and left hand. In using the left hand, every facet described above is reversed. The hook shot should be practiced from the low post position. It should be practiced using one dribble into the lane and one dribble down the lane. Again, use of both hands is a must.

Diagram 5.1
The Hook Shot

Turn-Around Jumper. Most coaches are aware of the basic fundamentals of the *jump shot*. For the post man, it is of maximum importance
to do a few more things in shooting the turn-around jumper. First
and foremost, he must not make himself small by bringing the pass
which he has received down to his waist or below the waist. The
defensive guards thrive on this. The good post man, after receiving
his pass, must keep the ball up chest high or higher. If he has received
a lob pass above his head, it is crucial for him to keep the ball there on
the pivot and on the shot.

Secondly, the post man must read the defense properly in order
to be in a position to shoot the turn-around jumper. After receiving the
pass, he thrusts his head toward the baseline. ONLY if he sees a man
directly in his path does he begin to think "turn-around jumper." If
he does not see a defensive man directly in his line, he is going to
power to the basket. In initiating the pivot to shoot the turn-around,
the post man must be instructed to be QUICK BUT NOT IN A
HURRY. The pivot is a quick, not a slow, deliberate one. As the pivot
begins, the ball remains firmly in control in the chest area—the
protective area of the body.

Thirdly, the post man must recognize the angle at which he is
to shoot the ball. If he has pivoted into the lane, he is to shoot the ball
directly over the front rim. If he is outside of the lane—one step off
the low or mid post areas—he is to use the backboard. This is crucial
for the other members of the team as they jockey for rebound position.
The post man must shoot the hook shot consistently off the board
when outside the key and consistently straight in over the front rim
when inside the key. It is important for us, as coaches, to demand that
players adhere to these principles and practice them daily.

In summary, after receiving the ball, the first thing the post man
has to do is to look over the baseline shoulder. If a defender is not
directly in front of him, he POWERS to the basket. No more than
one dribble is to be taken on this move.

If a defender is directly in front, the post man executes a quick
step to the middle for a short hook or a quick pivot to the middle for
the turn-around jumper. The confidence and ability of the post man in
executing both of these moves determines which one he will favor.

If a weak forward comes to the post man as he pivots or turns to
the middle, he passes the ball quickly opposite and then follows his
pass across the lane. See Diagram 5.2.

A post man who has a power layup, a hook into the middle, or a
turn-around jumper can operate very effectively from the multi-purpose

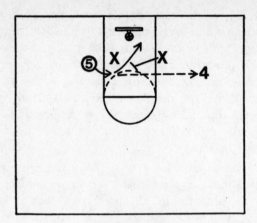

Diagram 5.2

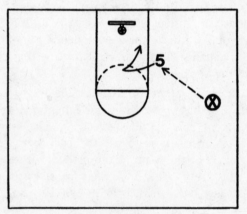

Diagram 5.3

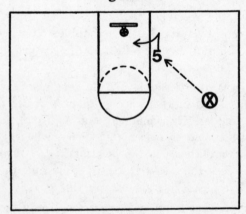

Diagram 5.4

area. Of course, an integral part of the move is the ability to be able
to recognize defenses and to pass the ball off to a teammate who is
open. Spin moves and cross over moves as shown in Diagrams 5.3 and
5.4 should also be taught. These are used to combat sagging defenses,
double teams, and a quick moving defensive post man who is constantly shifting. But if one masters the three basic shots, these others
flow naturally from them and make the post man very difficult to handle.

HIGH POST MOVES

After learning the moves in the multi-purpose area at the low or
middle post, the post man must know what to do with the ball should
he come to the high post to receive the ball. From the free throw line
(high post), the post man must be able to execute a number of moves
facing the basket. This practice is sometimes very trying to both coach
and post man, because many post men have played very sparingly while
facing the basket or "squared up" with the basket.

There are two basic ways for the high post man to react after he
receives the pass at the free throw line. First, he may pivot, face the
basket, and then make his move. Secondly, he may drop step, drive, and
shoot a wide variety of shots.

The drop step, drive move is particularly effective against a defender
who rushes up to play the post man who has broken to the ball. After
several times of having pivoted on the defender and going off a rocker
move, a quick drop step often leaves the defensive post men standing.
For this reason, it is imperative to emphasize the pivot turn move *first*.

The pivot-face moves are simple. A quick pivot-turn upon reception
of the pass and a quick reading of the defense tells the post man if he
should shoot the jumper immediately, drive to the bucket, or pass to a
teammate. If the post man is late defending or off by a step, the turn-
around jumper is in order. If the defender is all over the post man, a
dribble drive move is what is needed. If the drive is cut by a weak-side
defender who comes over to double up, then a quick pass-off is necessary.

In teaching the drop-step moves, emphasis should be placed on the
following: drop-step, drive-power layup; drop-step, drive, spin, hook;
drop-step, drive, short jumper.

Drop-Step, Drive, Power Layup. As the post man breaks high and
receives the pass, he immediately fakes over his left shoulder, keeping
his left foot still. He then drops his right foot down the lane, puts the ball
down on the floor with the left hand, takes two dribbles—tough, power
dribbles, and jump stops off both feet. He then—with or without a

pump fake— powers to the basket for a possible three point play. The crucial coaching point is summarized in the phrase: "Be quick but don't hurry or rush." The player, while head faking over his left shoulder, must be conscious of NOT moving the left foot. This makes the move.

Drop-Step, Drive, Spin, Hook. The post man breaks to the ball and receives it properly. He fakes over his left shoulder, keeping the left foot still. He then drops his right foot down the lane and puts the ball down solidly on the floor off the dribble with the left hand. However, he realizes that he has been cut off by the defense and is unable to get into layup position. He suddenly plants the right foot, spins into the middle with the left foot, places the toes of his left foot toward the sideline, pushes off and shoots the right handed hook shot. The coaching emphasis should be placed on PLANTING the foot, getting a good bend from the left knee, maintaining good balances and getting adequate lift.

Drop-Step, Drive, Short Jumper. This move is the same as the other two with the exception that, after one dribble and a quick determination that the defender has cut off the path to the basket, the post man stops, squares up and shoots the baby jumper.

All three moves must be practiced using the left and right hands, moving down the left side of the lane and the right side of the lane.

POST PASSING

After receiving the ball, the post man should know what to do with it. He has three basic options: shoot, dribble, or pass. Which he does will depend on the game situation, the score, whether he is freer to shoot than a teammate, his range and that of his mates. The post man must be adept at passing. A post man who can both shoot and pass is a tremendous offensive weapon. The post man should work hard every day on perfecting his passing skills.

In breaking down post passing, the coach must be aware of creating in practice the game situations that confront the post man under competition. These situations must be worked on daily. For the post man it is much more important to recognize passing situations than to work and concentrate on passing form. Most of the time, the post man's pass will be a simple flick-of-the-wrist pass, a quick overhead pass, or maybe even a shovel pass. Therefore, setting up the situations on a skeleton basis and then adding defensive players is the best method of teaching POST PASSING.

Return or Fill Pass. This situation involves a player passing the ball to the post man and then filling an empty area below the line of the pass. See Diagram 5.5. The post man must be schooled in the key of recognizing when to hit the man who is filling. The key is this: when the defender playing the passer sags off to play the post man and does not follow his man toward the baseline.

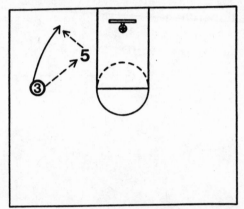

Diagram 5.5

Split of the Post Pass. This is a basic maneuver used by most teams. The ball is passed into the post man and the passer and another player split or scissors off the post. The post man must protect the ball on this, as well as any, maneuver by chesting it. His pass to a cutting teammate is a shovel pass. It is not a handoff. As the cutter streaks by, the post man gives him a simple underhand, shovel flip pass with a slight upward movement of his arms and ball. The point of emphasis here is on the shovel pass. If you do not demand this type of pass and allow the handoff, turnovers will result. See Diagram 5.6.

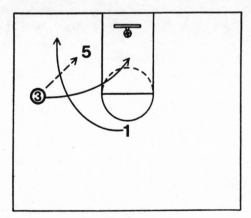

Diagram 5.6

The Flare Pass. The flare man is always the guard at the top of the circle. When the ball is passed into the post man from a wing position, the guard's first move is away toward the weak side. After reading the situation, the guard then moves to the weak-side free throw line extended. The post man, having been schooled in this maneuver, gives him almost a blind over-the-head pass and the guard gets a wide-open jumper. Or, if the post man will follow his pass, there is an easy layup awaiting the cutting post man. See Diagram 5.7.

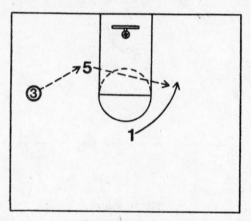

Diagram 5.7

Back Door or Weak-Side Pass. Against a team that sags its weak-side men, this pass is most effective. It is also good against overplaying defenses and against spread defense when the offensive team is in its delay game. As the post man receives the ball, he senses a weak-side man doubling up on him. He then "bullets" the ball to an opposite wing man who expects the pass. The same situation is created by the post man turning toward the middle for a short hook and spying the

Every team must be a master of the basic back door pass to a cutting weak-side guard and a back door pass to an overplayed strong-side forward. Diagram 5.9 shows the pass to the guard. Diagram 5.10 shows the pass to the cutting forward.

The basic pass is a bounce pass. Post men, bigger men in general, have trouble executing the bounce pass. They tend to release the pass too far up from the floor, resulting in a very high bounce and a very difficult pass to handle. The coaching secret to this play and the pass is to make the post man get down with bent knees as close to the floor with his release as possible. Also, demand that he know good angles. The execution takes countless hours of practice. But the rewards are great as layups come frequently off this maneuver.

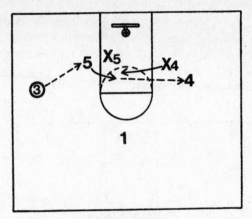

Diagram 5.8

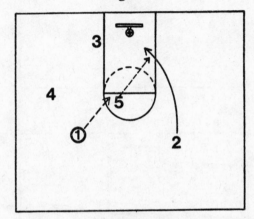

Diagram 5.9

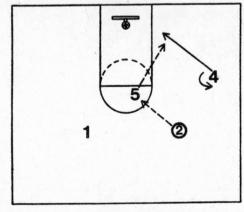

Diagram 5.10

Buddy Pass. Every post man should have a buddy on the court—a forward whom he looks for every time he gets the ball inside. The "buddy" always uses the same basic move—a quick flash or loop move into the middle of the lane from the low post area. Generally, you will find two players who read each other and pass the ball to each other well on every team. See Diagrams 5.11 and 5.12.

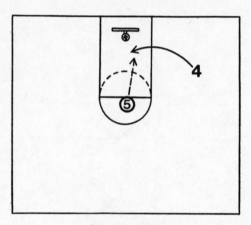

Diagram 5.11

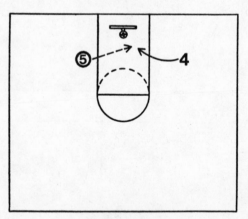

Diagram 5.12

This pass and move is very effective when the post man is a definite triple threat and the entire defense is geared to stopping him. It also scores often from a 1-3-1 alignment. The pass is a simple quick flip or lob pass, sometimes even a quick bounce pass. The key is timing and knowledge—knowledge that the post man's buddy will be in the assigned place when certain variables have been met.

All of these passes are drilled first from a skeleton basis. They are excellent as a pre-practice shooting-passing combination drill to loosen up the players before the actual scrimmage takes place. Some teams even use these as part of their pre-game warmup.

After the basic footwork and knowledge is gained, then defenders are placed in the drill. With the defense varying its tactics, the post man is put to the real test of reading and using all of the skills mentioned in this and other chapters.

6

SECRETS OF DEVELOPING
THE POST REBOUNDER

THEORIES ON REBOUNDING

Rebounding has been called the "blood area" of basketball, the "war zone," the "proving ground" among other phrases. No matter what one labels it, there is little doubt that REBOUNDING determines the outcome of many basketball games. The team that dominates on the boards, at both ends, will win most of its games.

There have been many theories on rebounding. Some coaches teach the straight block out with specific emphasis on a front or a reverse pivot. Others teach no block out at all. "Just go get the ball" is the admonishment from those coaches who adhere to this theory. Still others advocate opening to the ball, giving the defense a line to the basket, and then taking that line away from him. There are countless more.

I have gone through all of these theories. Most are based on the idea of contact and then, after holding the man for a count, going to the ball. Most theories are built around jumping. And coaches have continually emphasized jumping and leg development in connection with rebounding. I even went so far, in my early career as a coach, to contact a ballerina to give advice and a series of leg exercises to my players. After all, who has better developed legs and better co-ordination than a ballet dancer?

I've gone through all of the above theories, taught all of the "IN" techniques to my players. We've jumped rope daily, worked on leg development with the Universal Gym Machine, did toe and heel raises, and the like. But I still felt dissatisfied. I still watched my teams be only mediocre in the rebounding department. I watched my players —who *were* good jumpers and did box out and did possess nice, strong-looking legs—still not be able to secure the ball off the boards.

All of this led me to believe that maybe I had emphasized the wrong thing. Yes, you have to learn to jump with your legs. Yes, you must block out. But you gain possession with your arms and hands. And next to positioning. I slowly became aware that perhaps the next most important component of rebounding was the arms.

What conviction I needed, what proof I desired, came from an analysis of photos, pictures, and stop-action TV shots of "war under the boards." I watched Bill Walton—great star of the N.B.A.—perform. It is easy to remember him running downcourt with arms hoisted in the air, slipping inside or outside of people on the court, dodging would be defenders, but always with his arms UP.

I became particularly cognizant of photos of players battling for the ball on the boards. I began to notice a trend in the position of their arms. The goal of all good rebounders appeared to be the same in all pictures: free the arms, and try to lock or pin the arms of the opponent to his body. If a player can keep his opponent from lifting those arms up above his head, it is a virtual impossibility to secure a rebound. Yes, one must learn to jump with his legs, but one gains possession with the arms and hands. Perhaps we coaches have emphasized the wrong anatomical part of the body in trying to develop good rebounders. Since most rebounders are taken below the rim anyway, instead of leg emphasis, perhaps it should be arm and upper body emphasis.

After some testing and experimentation, I became convinced that the "arms up" emphasis was correct. So we began to teach a semi-modified traditional approach to rebounding. Upon the shot, we did block out by making contact with our opponent. We did not emphasize or even care what kind of pivot was employed, much less if a pivot were employed at all. Our arms were supposed to be thrust into the air as soon as the shot went up. We were to raise them higher than our opponent's. If possible, we try to place our elbows over our opponent's upper arm and shoulder, thus pinning him down. Our butt was down, our back arced. But our major emphases became: free the arms and raise them. We then taught our players to jump with a slight rotation of the hands. Most rebounds are not taken above the rim anyway, so height of jump becomes minimized. Most post men are capable of touching the rim. Thus, positioning and the "arms up" theory became most important for us.

PHYSICAL DEVELOPMENT OF THE
POST REBOUNDER

With the theory of rebounding now well defined, our early practice sessions see us spend a lot of time on "GETTING PHYSICALLY READY" to rebound. This, in turn, is the time for us to really develop the tough habit of raising those arms up in the air upon an attempted field goal. I want to stress here that the arms-up position is not a natural one. Most players are accustomed to cupping the defensive man around the thighs to hold him from the boards. Some players are advanced enough to keep the arms up, but only parallel to the shoulders. We want the arms up in the air to the point where the elbows are at eye level.

In developing the theory into practice, it is very important to do two things at the outset.

1. Prove to your players that their arms are less developed than the legs, and they need to work hard on upper body development. We do this by having two players stand next to a wall. One has a ball, the other does not. We tell player A, with the ball, to extend his arms above his head and dribble or pitty-pat the ball against the wall. His arms should be fully extended as he does this. He is only 4-5 inches away from the wall. See Diagram 6.1.

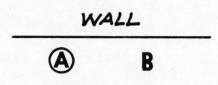

Diagram 6.1

We tell player B, without the ball, to jump as long as he can without stopping.

We then ask the rest of our squad which player will wear out first? Will it be PLAYER A, who is tipping or dribbling the ball on the wall above his head? Or will it be PLAYER B, who is jumping?

Invariably there will be some disagreement among the players as to who will falter. But the end result of the experiment is always the same. PLAYER A, with his arms upraised, will always tire before PLAYER B. The reason is simple enough. Players' legs have been developed to a greater degree than the arms. The arms tire more quickly, and hence we have proven our point: all players need upper body and arm development, more so than leg development.

2. Point #2 is one of terminology. Having established the fact that arm development is necessary, it is important to have all players understand our theory of rebounding and what we want them to do.

So, we will explain our rebounding communicative phrases that will be employed to teach our technique. These phrases are three:

1. THE WORK POSITION—this is proper rebounding position with the arms raised above the shoulders.
2. THE REST POSITION—this is a position whereby the arms are parallel to the shoulders. The player here is "resting."
3. THE LAZY POSITION—this is any position in which the arms are below the shoulders. Most often this is the position where the arms are near the opponent's thighs.

I emphasize here that I want my players, through repetition and practice, to develop the good habit of always rebounding in the WORK POSITION.

DRILLS TO DEVELOP THE ARMS-UP HABIT

Many of the drills that we run daily are done with the arms in the work position.

1. **Wall Dribbling.** Every player will wall-dribble in the manner described. He will do this from 3-5 minutes a day. If a player is hurt with a leg or ankle injury, ask him to come up and do this exercise to keep those arms from weakening. We emphasize the locking of the elbows and maintenance of good work position at all times.

2. **Continuous Jumping.** Though jumping is not the major point of emphasis in rebounding techniques, it is still important to work on the legs daily. BUT JUMP WITH ARMS LOCKED ABOVE THE HEAD IN THE WORK POSITION. Start about three minutes of continuous jumping in this position and eventually work up to ten or twelve minutes. Vary the time daily; and often, to break the monotony that sets in with the drill, pipe music into the gym or have the players hold a ball above their heads or even allow conversation.

3. **Running the Lines.** As most teams do, have your players run the lines—end line, free throw line, 10 second line, end. See Diagram 6.2. But have them run these with their arms up above their heads. On a normal 90 foot court, a running time of 28 seconds is excellent. If a player fails to run the lines in the allotted time, make him do it again.

4. **Over the Top Tipping.** Two players stand—one on each side of the basket—and tip the ball back and forth to each other, never allowing their arms to descend from the WORK POSITION.

5. **Three Man Tipping Rotation.** Three men line up as shown in Diagram 6.3 and tip the ball across the board. After tipping, the player slides or rotates in the manner described—clockwise. Again, ARMS UP AT ALL TIMES, even while sliding or rotating. Recall that the main purpose of these drills is to begin to develop the habit of raising

the arms and then keeping them above the head while working for
the rebound.

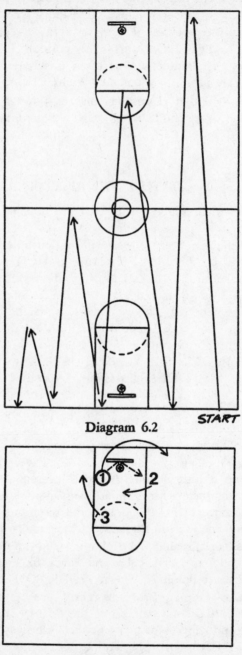

Diagram 6.2   START

Diagram 6.3

DEVELOPING THE HANDS

It is also important at this stage of development to work on the hands and fingers. After all, even though the arms are fully raised to grab the rebound, it is actually the HANDS AND FINGERS that do the work of securing and holding onto the ball.

The most-used exercise for the fingers is squeezing a rubber ball. This is good; but I really feel that, since our sport is basketball, as coaches we should have our players work as much as they can with THE BALL. Therefore, we have found that finger strength and hand-ball co-ordination are greatly helped by squeezing a basketball rather than a rubber ball. Our usual procedure is to get one of our older balls, one that will not be used by our squad in practice. We then deflate the ball slightly (assuming the player cannot palm it already). This slight deflation of the ball should be such that the person using the ball can with MAXIMUM, INTENSE effort eventually palm the ball. In this manner, we are increasing the player's finger strength, having him work with the basketball, helping him palm the ball—all three worthwhile accomplishments to the player's skill development. If the player can already palm the ball, we increase the air pressure in the ball above the maximum and tell him we want him to be able to palm the oversized ball. It is a unique concept. Try it.

The TOSS-BACK is a good mechanism for helping finger strength. Many of the passing drills are specifically designed to help this particular development. Finger-tip push-ups, wall-dribbling, and many of the Maravich ball-handling drills are also used in this development of finger/hand strength.

DEFENSIVE REBOUNDING DRILLS

There seems to be little doubt that the team that controls the backboard usually wins the game. It stands to reason that the man who almost always is in a position to rebound is the man who plays in the KEY or LANE position—the post man. So even though the drills, exercises, and techniques mentioned in this and other chapters can be applied to all players, it is almost mandatory that they BE applied to your POST MEN.

In developing good, aggressive defensive rebounders, we use a rather simple concept. We start by explaining the form. We then ask our players to go through "phantom" drills or simulations to check on form mastery. We then add a basketball to the one-man drills. We next add another player to make the drills TWO-MAN drills. Finally, and most importantly, we add multi-players to the drills. We spend most of our time on multi-player drills since most rebounds are grabbed in a crowd anyway. So we work hard on the idea of rebounding "in a crowd."

In our phantom drills, we ask each player to pretend that he is going for the rebound. We want him to leap in the air with arms extended, snatch the ball in mid-air, come down in what we call "spread eagle" fashion—butt out, legs spread, back arched, elbows extended as ball is protected in the chest area. Once we are convinced that the player has the technique we want, we then let him throw the ball off the board and go get it, without any opposition, in the fashion described. We emphasize SOUND here: we want to hear the player grunt as he goes up and grabs the ball. We want to hear the sound of the flesh of the hand pounding against the leather of the ball. And finally, we want to hear the loud thud of the feet as they ricochet to the floor in possession of the ball.

After we are satisfied with this phase of the individual's game, we then put him through what we call our "REBOUNDING BOTH SIDES OF THE BOARD" drill. The player stands outside the lane near the second free throw slot. He throws the ball off the board so that it caroms to the other side of the lane. The player must fly across the lane, leap into the air, snare the ball with both hands pounding the leather, land with a loud thud on the floor, and cradle the ball in the chest area with elbows extended. Both feet must be outside of the lane, in order to develop the proper foot movement and quickness necessary to get *every* carom. See Diagram 6.4.

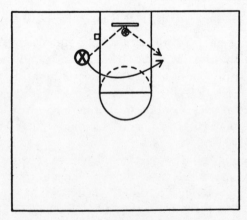

Diagram 6.4

With emphasis on good balance, the player repeats the same drill by tossing the ball off the board so that it angles to the other side. The player repeats this procedure for 30-60 seconds. It is important to rebound outside of the lane. The drill is an excellent conditioner and enables you to watch your rebounder's technique for a sustained period of time.

We also do a similar drill with the entire team. We have markings on the floor next to the wall—the markings being 12 feet apart. Every player has a ball and starts by throwing the ball off the wall in such a way that it caroms about 12 feet opposite, forcing the player to scurry over to grab the ball before it hits the floor. Thus, the players are performing the "BOTH SIDES OF THE BOARD" drill. The advantage of using the wall is that all players can work at once. The disadvantage is that the ball does not come off the wall in the same manner, angle, or velocity that it comes off the backboard.

Two-Man Drill.

As mentioned at the outset, we have emphasized the arms in our rebounding technique. This is not to say that we forgot completely about positioning or the legs. Our first two-man drill involves no basketball at all. It is our "BUTT TO BUTT" drill. The purpose of this is to emphasize proper positioning with the body and legs so that one can attempt to secure the ball with the arms. Two players are stationed in one of the three circles on the court. Their backs are arched against each other. They have a wide base, arms are up in the air fully extended. Upon the coach's whistle, each player drives the other with the buttocks, back, and legs and tries to force him out of the circle. Players must maintain good body balance, and yet push without the use of the arms. The players enjoy this drill and there is little chance of injury from it.

One-on-One Rebounding

Station the defensive player at various spots along the court with an offensive man right on his back. The coach will shoot the ball off the rim and both men will react to it. Both are instructed to thrust their arms up in the air and try to get to the boards. The defensive man with the inside position SHOULD secure the ball. Don't, however, stop play with possession. A total team game is based on quick conversion. Allow the rebounder to wheel out with a full head of steam and convert to the other end. The offensive player now becomes the defensive player, so he too is working on conversion.

Next run the same drill except that the defensive man will have a ball. Allow him to throw the ball against the board—making sure that the ball does go above the square on rectangular boards. It is a more difficult drill than the previous one for the defensive man because there is less reaction time on the part of the defensive rebounder—he has to throw the ball up, check his man, get the arms up in the air, and go get the ball. This adds a bit of quickness to the entire rebounding process. All through these activities, allow for contact and encourage the offensive man to nudge and lean against the defender. Finally, ask the man who secures the ball—hopefully the defender—to convert to offense while the other man converts to defense.

Two Ball Outlet Drill.

Another drill that involves two men in a game situation is the TWO BALL OUTLET DRILL. The setup of the drill is shown in Diagram 6.5. The drill is run in this manner. One of the shooters (1) shoots the ball, trying to score. "X" screens out "O". If the ball goes in, "X" the defensive rebounder grabs the ball from the net before it hits the floor and fires it full court to "5" who shoots the uncontested layup. If the initial shot were missed, depending upon which side of the floor the ball caroms to, "X"—the defensive rebounder—would outlet it to the proper outlet guard (3 or 4). The offensive rebounder—"O"—naturally adds a lot of pressure and resistance to "X" as he tries to do his job. After the defensive rebounder has outletted the ball, the opposite shooter fires the ball towards the basket. So basically, the shooters are alternating or taking turns shooting. As soon as the defensive rebounder has released his pass, another shot is on its way.

It is advisable to begin running this drill without an offensive rebounder. Simply allow the defensive rebounder to work hard snaring the ball and outletting it. He knows for certain that he will get the shot either made or missed. Generally keep X in the defensive rebounding position for as long as two to three minutes. This becomes a bear, especially if the shooters are hot. It is possible for the rebounder to have to hurl 15-20 full court passes in a minute. Fatigue really sets in. But this affords the coach a great opportunity to emphasize the arms-up technique when a rebounder is tiring. Keep the rebounder in the drill until he does it perfectly: that is, arms always up, constant effort, good anticipation where the rebound will carom, good rebounding form, good outlet, not allowing the ball to hit the floor. The drill is an excellent multi-purpose drill as shooters get good shooting practice, the release

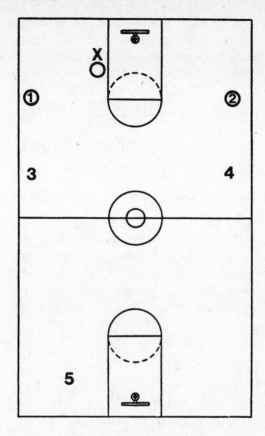

X   REPRESENTS DEFENSIVE REBOUNDER

O   REPRESENTS OFFENSIVE REBOUNDER

1-2 TWO PERIMETER SHOOTERS, EACH
     WITH A BASKETBALL

3-4 OUTLET GUARDS WHOM X WILL
     OUTLET THE MISSED SHOT TO

5   RELEASE GUARD WHO STREAKS
     DOWNCOURT ON EVERY SHOT

Diagram 6.5

man has to catch the full court pass and shoot the layup, and the rebounder and outlet guards are involved in pass timing. Needless to say,
the conditioning aspect for the rebounder is also very important. RE-
MEMBER. THE DRILL IS MIGHTY EFFECTIVE EVEN WITHOUT
SOMEONE CONTESTING THE REBOUNDER. BY ADDING AN
OFFENSIVE REBOUNDER, THE DRILL REALLY BECOMES
TOUGH. Work the post man in this drill daily. He is the main man
in any rebounding scheme, and his ability to rebound, outlet, grab the
made field goal, and pass is essential to most games.

Multi-Player Defensive Rebound Drill

As stated earlier, most rebounds are gathered or fought for in a
crowd. So most of the drills should be multi-player drills. Most coaches
do all of the three lane, three man rebounding drills. See Diagram 6.6.
But there are some rather novel and extremely effective drills to improve
defensive rebounding.

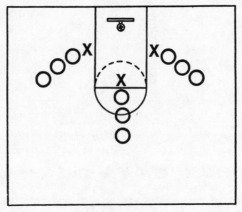

Diagram 6.6

Disadvantage Drills

The purpose of this series of drills is to put the defensive player at a
distinct disadvantage in numbers or positioning so that he has to work
extra hard to get the ball. These disadvantage drills stress the idea of
"rebounding in a crowd" which is at the core of rebounding techniques.

1. **1 vs 2 drill.** This drill is quite similar to others. The purpose
is for a defensive rebounder to go to the boards against two offensive
players, take the contact that ensues, come down with the ball, and then

convert to offense. After the defensive man tries to advance the ball up court and either gets off a shot or loses the ball, he must be prepared to convert back from offense to defense as the other men are coming back against him 2-on-1. To start the drill it is important to first make the two offensive men stay a step behind the defensive rebounder. See Diagram 6.7. The drill starts with the defensive rebounder throwing the ball off the boards and all three fighting for it.

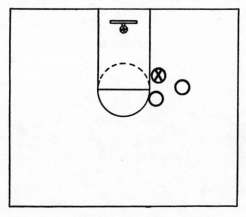

Diagram 6.7

2. **Wrong Side Drill.** Another excellent disadvantage drill that is effective is the WRONG SIDE DRILL. In this drill, hypothesize that the defensive man gets caught on the wrong side of the offensive man—in other words, the defender IS NOT between his man and the basket. The coach shoots the ball up and it is the job of the defensive men to correct the disadvantage and get back the inside position that they are supposed to have. If the offensive men get the ball, they go back up with it. If the defensive men get the ball, they convert to offense and try to score at the other end. See Diagram 6.8 for the initial lineup of the drill. Encourage the offensive players in this drill to recognize when they have inside position and try to block off the defensive man in the same manner that the defender would try to block them out if the situation were reversed.

3. **Block-out, Hustle, Reaction Drill.** A third effective disadvantage drill (the disadvantage drills are important because they are closer to game situations) is the block-out, hustle, reaction drill. The setup of this drill is shown in Diagram 6.9. The basic idea of the drill is for the defensive man (X) to react to the shot, block out one of the offensive men (#1 or #2), then react and play a shooter, and finally block

out and move to the boards again. The drill starts with the coach taking a shot and missing it. He calls out a number, #1 or #2. For explanation's sake, assume that the coach calls "#1." #1 then heads for the boards and the defender must block him out and get the rebound. As soon as the defender secures the ball he makes a crisp chest pass to the other offensive man who is off the free throw line extended. #2—the offensive man—may not dribble but must take a jump shot as the defender rushes out to get a hand in his face.

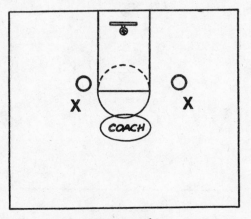

Diagram 6.8

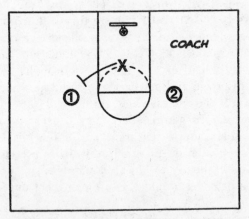

Diagram 6.9

Meanwhile the other offensive man (#1) has moved back to his spot free throw line extended. As soon as #2 releases his shot, #1 again heads for the boards. The defender, always thinking and reacting, has to hustle over and keep #1 from getting to the boards. See Diagram 6.10.

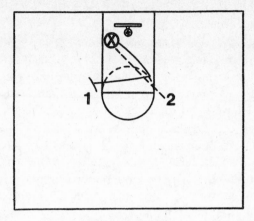

Diagram 6.10

This procedure is kept up until the coach feels that the defender has sufficiently hustled and rebounded with proper techniques. To end the drill, the coach simply yells "GET IT" and all three men crash the boards. This is an excellent disadvantage drill which combines intense hustle and reaction, besides quick thinking on the part of the defensive man.

4. **Meatgrinder.** For this drill put any number of players in the lane and tell them that they can get out of the drill by grabbing and outletting to the coach TWO rebounds. The coach shoots the ball and the players go after it. This is rebounding in a crowd at its best. It is important to realize that you should expect to see 16 arms (if 8 men are in the lane) up in the air as the shot goes up. There is to be no pushing with the hands. Players are encouraged to use their lower anatomy and legs to position self, but arms have to be up.

ZONE REBOUNDING DRILLS

There seems to be little doubt that many believe in a man-to-man defense because each defensive man has a definite responsibility on the boards—an assigned man to keep off. Zone defenses are often susceptible to being out-rebounded. If your players are well-schooled in the art of offensive rebounding, you can hurt the zone defense on the boards. To combat this weakness in the zone, it is imperative that drills be designed to emphasize zone defensive rebounding.

1. **2-Man Cross Block Out.** This is a 2-on-2 drill. But as the ball is shot, the defensive men must switch defensive assignments and block out the other's man. The drill is designed for good, quick foot reaction.

Vary the shooting spots and cover those areas where good zone offensive teams attack the zone.

2. **Rotation Triangle Drill and Rotation Rectangle Drill.** Both of these drills have the same idea as the CROSS BLOCK OUT. The three men form a triangle, but as the shot goes up, they must rotate clockwise or counterclockwise to rebound. When four men are added, place them in a rectangle and have them rotate on the shot. See Diagram 6.11.

All through these drills constantly stress to the players to BLOCK OUT SOMEBODY, TO REACT TO THE BALL, AND TO EVENTUALLY FORM THE REBOUNDING TRIANGLE—all ideas essential to any rebounding, but of utmost importance to zone rebounding. These secrets do work, but recall, any zone defensive team must admit to defensive rebounding deficiencies.

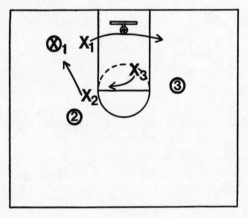

Diagram 6.11

OFFENSIVE REBOUNDING DRILLS

Offensive rebounding lends itself to much philosophy and theory. The defense has every advantage in the rebounding department. Because of the nature of the game, the defender is usually—almost always—between his man and the basket and hence in a more favorable position than the offense. So, even if the offensive player does everything that the coach has told him, it is not a sure-fire thing that he will get the ball. In fact, if the defensive man is well-schooled in his art, the chance of gathering in the ball is remote.

Good offensive rebounding is often created by good movement on offense to keep the defense in motion. Good offensive rebounding techniques demand intense concentration and maximum effort on the part of the offensive player. The good offensive rebounder NEVER gets himself blocked out; he'll go anywhere to get open and make a path to the boards for himself. He knows where the ball most likely will carom to, when shot from a specific spot. He will do anything to get a hand on the ball to keep it alive.

As far as teaching goes, we want our players to do one of four things to get away from the defensive rebounder who is trying to block him out.

1. Try to get a leg across the man who is trying to block you out. With the leg first across, then pull the head and shoulders through. It is always imperative to keep the hands and arms up—higher than the defensive man's. Hard rebounds, long rebounds, and the chance to get a fingertip on the ball are all enhanced by arms-up technique.

2. Initiate a back spin and roll off the defender to one side or the other. This move is effective because it causes confusion on the part of the defender.

3. Fake and try to go opposite. Try to get the defender to watch you, to worry about your movement a split second longer than he wants to.

4. If nothing else works and the defender is especially tenacious, simply slide him outside of the prime rebound areas and take him right out of the play. In this case, let your teammates do the rebounding. We often use this to pull a good, but rather slow-thinking rebounder away from his game.

To develop offensive rebounding moves and techniques, we have our post men perform daily our SUPER 11 SEQUENCE. At times we ask our forwards to do these also. But this is *mandatory* for our post man *daily*.

Super 11 Sequence

1. REBOUND BOTH SIDES OF THE BOARDS, This drill was described earlier. The player lands with both feet outside of the lane, tosses the ball off the board, and retrieves it with good form on the opposite side of the lane. We do 10 on each side.
2. TIPPING RIGHT/LEFT. Next our post man will toss the ball off the board, tip it 10 times, and then tip it in. He will go opposite and do the same thing, using the other hand.
3. RACE AND TIP. The player aligns himself as shown in

Diagram 6.12. He tosses the ball off the boards with an under-handed flip and races in to tip it. He grabs the ball, runs to the other side of the court, and repeats. We do 5 on each side.

4. RIP AND POWER. Player stands at second free throw slot, tosses ball up, "RIPS" it down with spread eagle form, then after regaining good body balance, POWERS the ball back up. We do 10 on each side.

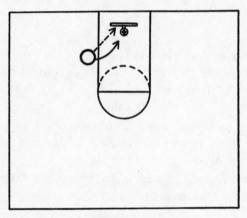

Diagram 6.12

5. RIP-FAKE-POWER. This drill is the same as #4, except that when the player comes down and gathers himself, he gives a good quick head-pump fake, and then POWERS. 10 on each side.

6. RIP-STEP UNDER. Player throws ball off board. Comes down. Steps underneath to the other side of the hoop and buttonhooks it in.

7. RIP-FAKE-STEP UNDER. Same as above, but add a fake before stepping under.

8. RIP and HOOK. Throw ball off board, rip it down, and short hook in middle. 10 on each side.

9. HAND TOUGHENER. Throw ball off board, grab above the rim, and hit the ball against the rim as you come down with it. (Only bigger players will be able to do this.) Repeat 10 times.

10. TWO BALL DUNKS. Coach or manager places two balls on rectangles at first free throw slot along the lane. Player picks ball up and dunks as many as he can, alternating sides, until fatigued.

11. SUPER SLAM. Player starts at 3-4 free throw slot extended, tosses ball off the board underhanded at such an angle that

it will carom over the front rim. He races into the middle and slam-dunks it. Smaller players can tip it in. Repeat 5-10 times from both sides. See Diagram 6.13.

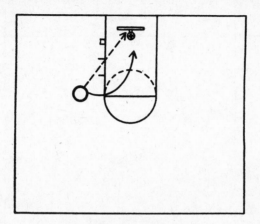

Diagram 6.13

This entire sequence of 11 can be accomplished after a few practice runs in about 12 minutes, depending upon the skill and hustle of the player involved AND the number of repetitions for each drill. We have found that the SUPER ELEVEN accomplishes quite a few things. It improves jumping, timing, and co-ordination. It definitely helps offensive rebounding techniques: quick movement and reaction, tipping, power moves, faking, and the like. Finally, it does build stamina, strength and endurance. Our post men do these daily, our other players when we feel the need.

Offensive Tipping

Since we stress to our players that they must get at least a hand on the offensive rebound, we do emphasize tipping the basketball. Good arm extension with the elbow locked and fingers extended is the technique taught. We tip the ball with a slight bend of the wrist and a quick flick with the fingers. The three men tipping rotation is a good drill to teach offensive tipping and reaction. The normal tipping lines are useful but what about using full court line tipping? Five or six players line up at each basket as shown in Diagram 6.14. After tipping the ball, the player must hustle to the other end of the court and get in that line.

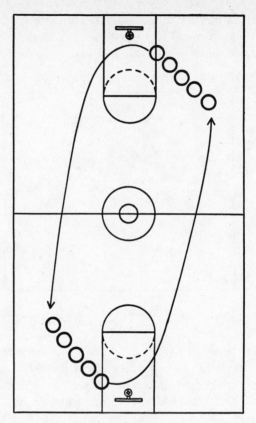

Diagram 6.14

Offensive Obstacle Course

The purpose of this drill is to force the offensive rebounder to react to defenders (obstacles) in his path, to keep his head up and YET get to the boards quickly enough to get a tip at the ball. Use football standing dummies or chairs as obstacles and switch the player around to different positions on the court. The ball is shot and the player must knife his way through the obstacles, ARMS UP AT ALL TIMES, and reach the ball before it hits the floor. He must not knock down or make contact with any of the obstacles. Time each player with a stopwatch. See Diagram 6.15.

REBOUNDING AND THE THINKING MAN

It is very important to think and to be observant in order to be a good rebounder. A player must play all the percentages in order to put himself into a position to get the ball. Such things as checking the tightness of a rim prior to the game and noticing how wide and long the court is are important. There are certain truisms that apply to the missed shot and the ensuing rebound. Players must be aware of these points. These are the author's opinions after documenting missed shots in various games.

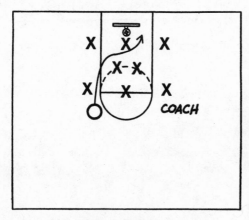

Diagram 6.15

Distance

    1. 10 - 15 ft. shots that are missed usually rebound short.

    2. 15 - 25 ft. shots missed usually rebound long.

Arc

    1. Shots with little arc are known as "hard shots" and usually rebound long and straight.

    2. Shots with high arc usually rebound high off the rim and fairly long.

    3. Shots with average arc—shots coming from the really good shooters—usually rebound softly and at the angle from which they were taken.

Angle

    1. Corner shots sometimes come back towards the shooter but usually carom to the opposite corner.

    2. Shots taken from the middle of the court return to the middle.

3. Shots taken from the side at a 45 degree angle usually rebound according to the arc and the force with which taken.

Time and Game Situation

1. As the game progresses, more shots are short than long. Hence, they will carom a little harder and longer off the front rim.
2. In a 4th quarter GAME SITUATION, if a shot is missed, it too will most likely be short.

Personnel

1. It is important to know the shooting traits and habits of each player on the opposing team: areas of best percentage, arc, range, etc.

Only by playing all the percentages, especially at the offensive end, can a player become a great rebounder and a team become a great rebounding team.

7

THE POST MAN
AND THE FAST BREAK

BUILDING THE FAST BREAK

Much has been written about the advantage of using a fast break type of offense. Besides the fact of heightened fan interest in a running game, the idea of controlling the tempo and always being in the game attracted many coaches to employ the break as their prime offensive weapon.

After making the decision to use the fast break, a coach has two important questions to answer for himself before he develops his break pattern and technique.

First, he must decide when to run. Should you run ALWAYS— after a missed field goal and after a made field goal? Should your run ONLY after a missed field goal? Or should you run ONLY in certain situations—when ahead by five or more, not in the last five minutes of a close game, when you have a numerical advantage?

Secondly, what type of initiation will be used to begin the break? Will it be an outlet pass to the sideline area? Or an outlet pass to a guard in the middle of the court at the top of the key? Will you release a guard long and try to "fly" the ball down to him if he is open? Will you allow your forwards and post man to dribble the ball out of trouble and bring it up in the middle on the break?

These questions and the answers you come up with are crucial before beginning to implement your post man into the break.

Integrating the post man into the fast break running game is a very difficult task, especially if he is big and slow or somewhat unco-ordinated. As indicated in previous chapters, the post man must be a strong rebounder and a smart passer. He must be able to outlet the ball after securing it off the boards. He must be taught the proper rebounding "turn." He must be taught to turn outside and never inside (see Diagrams 7.1 and 7.2).

When a rebounder turns inside as in Diagram 7.2, he is allowing the defense to converge upon him. There is simply too much congestion to initiate the break with a solid outlet pass.

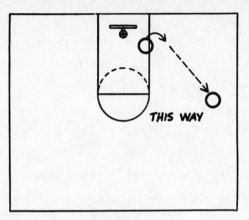

Diagram 7.1

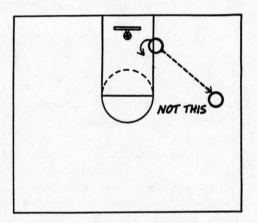

Diagram 7.2

Once the post rebounder has mastered the techniques of securing the ball and outletting it, it is important to get the post man RECOGNIZING, RUNNING, AND CATCHING. The drills employed to teach the fast break must be designed to emphasize, for post men, these three skills.

I feel that one of the most fundamental and most successful drills in all of basketball is the three lane full court running and passing drill. Working on this drill every day will pay handsome dividends for a running team. The three-lane drill combines running, passing, catching, and proper timing—all essential to the fast break. Teams like to vary the straight line running drill with a weave. This, too, is an excellent drill for the post man.

Prior to teaching the three-lane full-court running/passing drill, it is important to teach all players, but especially the post man, the proper way to cut. Assuming the post man is coming down the wing or sideline area on a break, teach him to begin his cut at the top of the key (see Diagram 7.3) by planting firmly the outside foot—in this case, the right foot—bending slightly at the knees. As the right foot is firmly planted, the head leans forward slightly, and the right arm and hand (with clenched fist) are thrust forward, creating a good and effective head and shoulder fake. (In trying to visualize this imagine a one-hundred yard sprinter propelling himself from the starting blocks.)

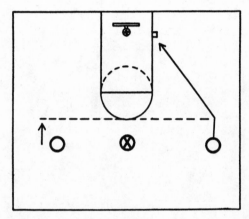

Diagram 7.3

With the body under proper control, the left leg is suddenly thrust in the opposite direction towards the basket. The left foot is planted firmly on the floor. The foot is then used for good leverage as the player pushes off the left and begins his quick movement to the basket.

In order to develop this technique under the watchful eye of the coach, set up the court as shown in Diagram 7.4 with tape marking the "X" spots. The post man starts at the designated spot and proceeds to "SPRINT AND CUT" slowly, at first, under the coach's watchful eye. The emphasis is placed on proper timing and proper footwork—the planting of the outside foot on the "X" mark, the effective arm, head, shoulder fake, and the thrusting of the other leg in the opposite direction. It's not as easy as it looks and it does help build leg co-ordination.

After teaching the proper cutting technique, expect the post man and all players to use such cuts in running the full court 3-lane drill or the full court 3-lane weave drill. Demand perfection in cutting and timing. It will pay off in getting the good layup shots on the break.

Another point of emphasis on the three lane full court drill is to make certain that the cutters cut to the high side of the box—not below it, to the low or baseline side. To emphasize this, put a chair, a football tackling dummy, or another player on the lane at the box and make all cutters cut in front on him. Too often cutters get themselves in trouble by cutting below the box. They are then forced to make a "prayer" shot in order to score. The proper angle is essential in shooting the layup off the fast break.

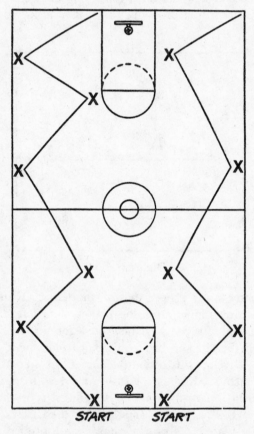

Diagram 7.4

In order to get the post man running and filling the lane, the following two drills are effective.

Rebound and Go Drill. The drill is set up with a post man in the lane as the rebounder and with a guard at the free throw line. A shot is taken and the guard moves to the outlet area on the side of the court to which the ball has rebounded. The post man secures the rebound and outlets the ball to the guard. The post man then either fills the opposite lane (Diagram 7.5) or follows his pass to the lane he has outletted the ball to (Diagram 7.6). Which method is employed depends on the coach's philosophy.

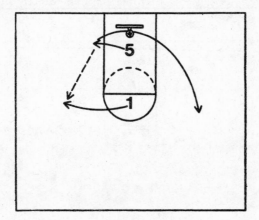

Diagram 7.5

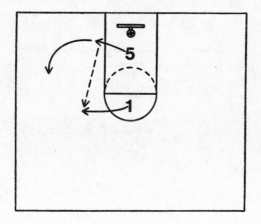

Diagram 7.6

In both cases the outlet guard (#1) dribbles into the middle. The post man sprints down the side to the top of the circle extended at the opposite end of the court, makes a good cut, and blasts in to receive a bounce pass from the guard. The post man then shoots the layup.

After some proficiency has been gained in the drill, put a defender in the lane and make the post man screen him out as the shot goes up.

The defender contests the post man as he tries to outlet the pass.

Another variation is to put a defender on the guard (see Diagram 7.7). Now guard #1 has to free himself and the post man (#5) must hit him with a perfect outlet pass. Or, if your philosophy so dictates, you can now have the post man— after he has cleared the boards and looked to the outlet area—dribble the ball directly into the middle himself and lead the break.

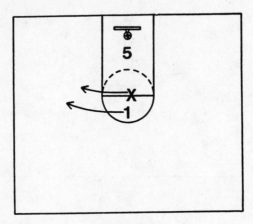

Diagram 7.7

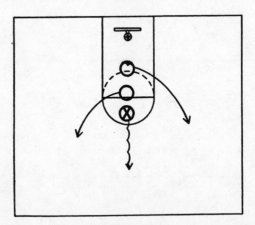

Diagram 7.8

Recognize, Race and Fill. This drill is set up with three men in a direct line at the free throw line. The first man in line has a ball and the third or last man in line is the POST MAN. The drill begins with the first man in line taking a few dribbles down the middle of the court. The second man fills either lane and the post man (the last man in the line) must sprint as hard as he can to fill the open lane because he will be on the receiving end of a bounce pass at the other end of the court for a layup. Besides the obvious, the drill is an excellent conditioner for the post man.

BREAKING WITH THE BIG POST MAN

A fast break, with a big, talented post man, must be predicated on getting the ball inside if the primary break is not there. Since, as indicated in previous chapters, a big, strong post man generally operates at the low post and uses power moves most of the time, an effective fast break attack with such a post man will have him enter the break at the low post position and try to maintain that position along either block. Assuming that the post man in the multi-purpose rebounding area has not filled one of the lanes on the primary break, he then becomes a trailer and is an integral, even focal, point of the secondary break. Hence, the discussion of the fast break and the post man is most often a discussion of the post man's role as a trailer in the secondary break!

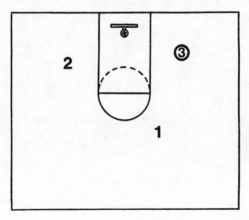

Diagram 7.9

There are many ways to use the post man in a fast break pattern. The one described here has been most successful for me. As the primary wave of the break attack is shut off, the ball is placed in one of two positions: (1) wing man (lane man) has the ball near the baseline (see Diagram 7.9); (2) middle man veers off to either side of the key (see Diagram 7.10).

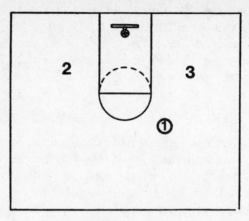

Diagram 7.10

The post man and usually one of the forwards are the trailers on the break. The rule for the trailers is always the same: the post man—no matter what side of the court he is trailing on—cuts first to the box opposite the ball. The wing man on that side of the court then clears the area by coming out to the guard position. The other trailer slows down and literally holds his position. (See Diagram 7.11).

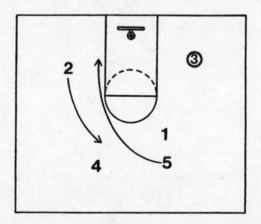

Diagram 7.11

The wing man with the ball (#3) should be looking over the top for the high lob pass to the post man (#5).

If nothing has developed after the post trailer cuts to the weak side, he hesitates for one count on the box and then flashes hard across the lane to the strong side. As this happens, the other trailer (#4) cuts to fill the spot vacated by the post man. (See Diagram 7.12.)

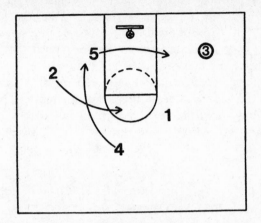

Diagram 7.12

An unchanging rule follows: if the post man has not received the ball at this point, he will stay posted up on that side of the lane and that side will be cleared. This will be accomplished by the wing man on the strong side (#3) returning the ball to the point and clearing opposite. By studying Diagram 7.13, one can see the opportunities now afforded by this manevuer. The swing man (#3) may be open coming around #4's screen. Guard #1 can jam the ball back into the post man #5 as the side is cleared. Or, as the ball is moved around the perimeter, #5 can flash into the lane.

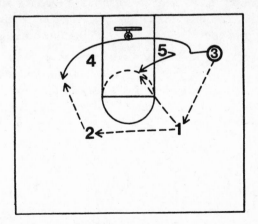

Diagram 7.13

This fast break maneuver utilizes the tall, strong post man. It places him in the area where he is most powerful—the low post, box area. For a small post man, especially against bigger people, this offensive maneuver might not be as effective. But the low post hook, the swing moves into the middle, and the inside power game are utilized by this fast break maneuver. The maneuver also presents some good scoring opportunities for the rest of the team. It is effective against both a man or zone defense. And finally, it is really a half court offense should the primary break not be there. For a running team who wants to constantly and relentlessly put pressure on the defense, for a running team that wants to utilize a big strong inside post man, this break movement is a natural and relatively simple one to master.

BREAKING WITH THE SMALL POST MAN

As alluded to before, the definition of a "big" post man and a "small" post man is relative to the geographical area, level of competition played, and to the talent around. A big post man might be a 6'2 kid if in that conference or geographical area most post men are 5'11 or 6'0. By the same token in some circles of competition, the 6'5 post man is a midget when his competition is 6'10 or above. So, again, the coach himself must determine what kind of post man he has and how he wants to use him.

If your post man has been labelled "small," you may assume that most of the times he will not be effective at the low post. So, why create situations where he will have to be overmatched down at the box areas. It stands to reason that a smaller post man must take advantage of his mobility, maneuverability, and quickness; these opportunities must be created for him in the secondary phase of the fast break attack.

Let us assume again that the primary break has not materialized in a basket. So now we see that the trailers of the secondary break have come into play. No matter how big or small the post man is, he still has to be run inside down the lane. This maneuver poses a threat—real or otherwise—and keeps the defense honest. No matter what the size of the offensive post man, he still has to be guarded when he flashes down low. So, as described earlier in the chapter, the secondary break maneuver will begin just as before, with the post man flashing opposite and then blasting hard across the lane towards the ball. See Diagram 7.14.

If he receives the ball at the low post, he must put on a move or kick the ball to an open man. If he doesn't receive the ball he slides up the lane and is prepared to step off the lane to a wing position in order to get it. Diagram 7.15 shows this maneuver. By stepping off the lane, the post man is now in a position to go 1-on-1 or to use his quickness in order to beat a taller foe. After #3 passes the ball to the post man, motion or passing game principles are employed. Should #3—the wing man—return the ball to the top of the key, the post man is then in a position to use a screen by #3 for a short jumper. Diagram 7.16 shows this move.

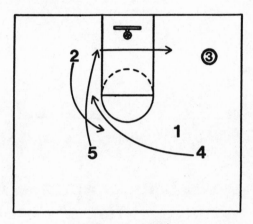

Diagram 7.14

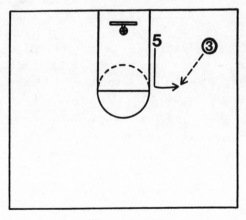

Diagram 7.15

Different coaches will have different moves to add to these maneuvers. However, the basic principle remains the same: if you have a big post man, keep him inside and force the defense to cover him at his strongest positions. If you have a smaller, more mobile post man, then

still post him up, but allow him the freedom to step off the lane or out
from the lane in order to utilize his assets.

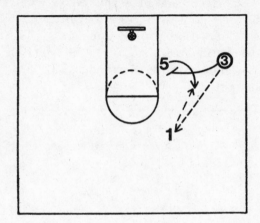

Diagram 7.16

TRANSITIONAL BREAK AND THE POST MAN

The transitional break is the break after a made field goal. As
mentioned previously, many fast break coaches do not like to run after
a made field goal. The feeling is that the defense has recovery time to
get back and build the defense. By forcing the ball upcourt against an
established defense, one would just be encouraging turnovers and poor
shots. However, the adherents of the transitional break counter by
citing game control and constant offensive pressure as the main reasons
to run at all times. The fast break coach *must* decide whether or not
to run after a made basket.

If you decide to run after a score, it is important to release a guard
on every shot. The release of a guard puts added pressure on the defense.
Few teams are able to send 5 men to the offensive boards anyway, so
rebounding will not be hampered by this move. It is also very difficult
to press a team that releases a guard on every shot.

In our scheme of things, our release guard always goes to the
right corner. Our second guard becomes the middle man of the break—
the man that we try to get the ball to after a made field goal. The left
lane will be filled by any one of the frontliners. Usually the post man
will be closest to the basket and get the ball out of the net to throw in.
A coach may or may not wish to designate him as the permanent in-
bounds passer. Once the ball is in-bounded, our break scheme is the

same as described earlier. Diagram 7.17 shows the maneuver, with #5—the post man—taking the ball out of the net. #4 and #5 then become the trailers in the secondary break.

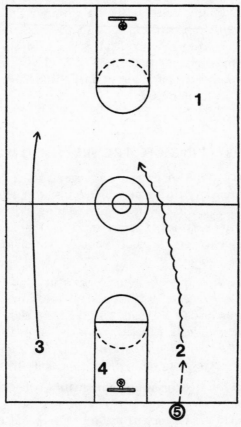

Diagram 7.17

Once in the offensive end of the court, the break takes on the same look as mentioned previously off the primary break. With a big post man, he flashes opposite and then comes to the ballside at the low post. With a smaller post man, he goes opposite and makes a good angle cut to the strong side. However, if he hasn't gotten the ball, he either slides up the lane and steps off or is prepared to get an inside screen to pop out on the wing position or baseline for a short jumper or a 1-on-1 move against the defense. By not changing much on the transitional break, a consistent teaching and learning mechanism has been maintained.

CONVERSION BREAK

A conversion break is a break after recovering a turnover—bad pass, steal, or the like. Since these recoveries occur anywhere on the court—offensive end or defensive end—this is more of a free-lance break than anything else. No definite rules can be set down for the post man. But, needless to say, with constant emphasis in practice upon the primary and secondary break after a missed field goal and constant emphasis on the transitional break after a made field goal, players tend to run the same pattern or maneuver off a transitional break if the easy layup is not there off a couple of passes.

BREAKING OFF THE FREE THROW

Another decision has to be made as regards the free throw break. Do you wish to run only after a missed free throw or after a made free throw, too? To run effectively off the free throw, it is necessary to be able to rebound the missed free throw and to get the made free throw out of the net before it hits the floor. Both of these must be worked on often in practice.

In keeping with simplicity of the break, the following free throw alignment best allows a team to run the same break free throw as off a missed field goal or made field goal. Diagram 7.18 shows the two best rebounders in the inside lane positions, with the guards in the next lane positions. A forward (#3) is back in the offensive end of the court. He will be the player to go to the right sideline and fill that lane.

At the end of the free throw attempt, guard #1 flares to the sideline at the outlet area to become the receiver, while guard #2 becomes the safety valve man. If the decision is made to attack the right side after a free throw, then the rebounder in the first rebound slot on the opposite side takes the ball out of bounds and out of the net. If the decision is made to attack the left side after a made free throw, then the rebounder on the opposite side will take the ball from the net. This procedure is employed because the rebounder coming across the lane has some momentum and doesn't have to turn his back to the play. He simply slides across the lane, catches the ball through the net, and steps out of bounds to fire. An easy way to key the side to be attacked is simply to designate an even number as the RIGHT SIDE, an odd number as the LEFT SIDE. The coach can signal this from the bench or the team captain can from the floor. Whatever side is attacked, the player that is back will always go to that side, and the guards will

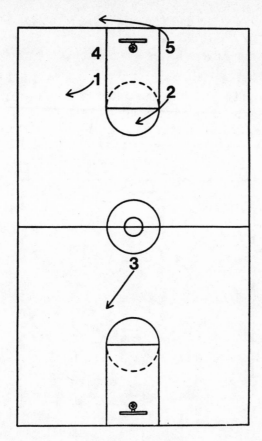

Diagram 7.18

man the middle and the opposite wing. The two inside rebounders are the trailers. So once again, the break attack doesn't vary that much from the primary and transitional breaks described earlier in the chapter.

A successful surprise maneuver off the made free throw—one that can be employed perhaps twice a game—is to screen for the post man and hustle him downcourt for an easy layup. This is set up by bringing the player who has set up in the front court up to the 10 second line. The forward takes the ball from the net and fires a basketball pass to the 10 second line, hitting the forward as he moves to the mid-court line. As shown in Diagram 7.19, guard #2 screens the defensive post man (#5) as the post man sprints down court.

The momentary screen by guard #2 only takes one-hundredth of a second. All he must do is detain the opposing center long enough for our post man to gain one step and begin his sprint. Particularly if the post man is big is this maneuver effective. Coaches can easily improvise other maneuvers off the made or missed free throw.

The fast break is a fun part of the game. Fans and players alike love to be involved in such a game. Intelligent use of the post man in such a style of play can lead to many easy baskets—off the rebound, off the turnover, off the made field goal, and off the made or missed free throw.

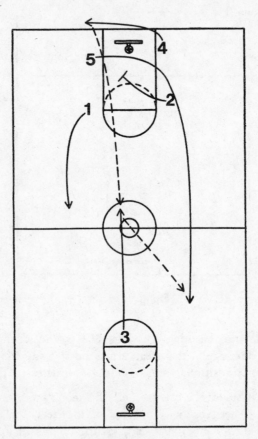

Diagram 7.19

8

POWER OFFENSES FOR
THE POST MAN

One of the most difficult jobs that a coach has each year is to evaluate his personnel to determine the placement of his players on the court. Especially at the non-collegiate levels, where coaches don't have as much to say about who is in their program, is this crucial to success. More often than not, a college coach or a professional coach can recruit or draft players to fit into a certain system and specific style of play. At the other levels of competition, a system or style of play has to be adapted to the players in the program. Therefore, more flexibility and perhaps even a wider knowledge of offensive systems and styles of play is necessary.

Recognizing a player's ability and getting the player to play within himself is the key to establishing a sound offensive system. A player must be convinced to try only to do those things that he is capable of doing. He should not try to be someone else or try to do something he can't do. Roles and recognition of roles are essential to success. A poor shooting but clever ball-handling guard should not try to score twenty-five points a game or gun the ball up from twenty feet. A small post man should not always try to muscle inside against bigger, stronger foes.

HIGH POST OFFENSE

Coaches should be able to structure both a high post offense and a low post offense. The ability of a coach to change his style of play and offensive system with changing personnel is the mark of a well-prepared coach. The development of an offense to utilize a post man who can shoot the ball from fifteen feet, or pass the ball well or screen or pick well, and even power inside is best accomplished from an alignment which starts the post man at a high post position along the free throw line. By placing the post man at the free throw lane, many more passing lanes are open to him. Another advantage of this placement is to spread out the defense and open more the middle of the lane.

To accomplish these goals, it is best to set up in a traditional 2-1-2 alignment (although this offense is easily adapted to a 1-3-1 or a 1-2-2). The movement is initiated by a guard-forward pass and a cut of the strong guard to the baseline off the post man. See Diagram 8.1. The weak-side players (#2 and #4) must be well-drilled in the movement of their defensive men.

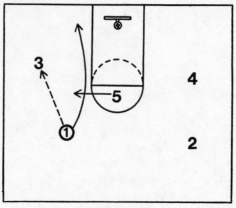

Diagram 8.1

The basic pattern continues with the forward passing the ball to the high post man who, after screening, steps off the lane and to the ball to receive a pass. Normally, the defensive center has to sag a bit to help cover the guard who is cutting through. This usually allows the post man to free himself. The weak-side forward (#4) moves his defensive man down to the low post box position and guard #2 executes a "flare" move as indicated in Diagram 8.2.

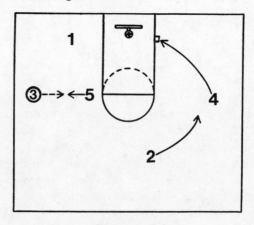

Diagram 8.2

The bread-and-butter moves now are executed. We have labelled them "UCLA" and "Laker." By definition, a "UCLA" move is a quick pop by the weak-side forward into the middle of the multi-purpose area. He tries to beat his defensive man. But if not, then the defensive man is usually in front and we can take advantage of this too. See Diagram 8.3.

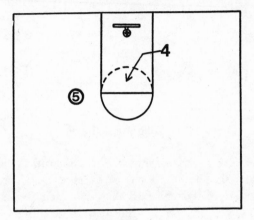

Diagram 8.3

By definition, "Laker" is nothing more than a baseline screen. See Diagram 8.4. So when the strong side forward passes the ball to the post man, the forward (#3) goes down to the baseline to execute a "Laker" screen for the guard who has cut through. Simultaneously, the weak-side forward, who has already moved his man to the low post box area, is executing a "UCLA" move against his man. Diagram 8.5 shows both moves.

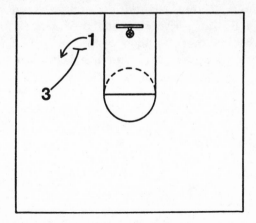

Diagram 8.4

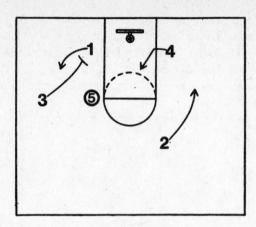

Diagram 8.5

A couple of keys to make these moves successful are necessary. The weak-side forward should not begin to execute his UCLA move until the post man has received the ball AND pivoted so he is facing the basket. The PIVOT is the key for the forward to move into the middle of the key. As far as the Laker move goes, it is mandatory that the guard (#1) set his man up so he runs him into the screen set by forward #3. Meanwhile, the off-guard, weak-side, "flares" to the free throw line extended. A good passing post man has five options. *First,* he looks for the UCLA man. This is the easiest shot. A good bounce pass if the defender is behind, or a crisp "halo" pass if the defender is fronting will result in an easy layup for the forward. The guard coming off the LAKER move is the *second* option. The forward who sets the screen on the LAKER move, after setting the screen, pivots and pins the defender on his back. Thus, he becomes the *third* option— and a good one at that should the defense switch. The weak-side guard who is "flaring" is the *fourth* option. And the post man shooting the jumper should the defense be sagging is the *fifth* option. Such a jumper is not a poor shot because there is ample board play underneath with the movement inside.

So far, this pattern has taken advantage of the post man's passing ability and shooting prowess from 15 ft. Using the post man as a screener is also an integral part of this pattern. Any time the post man hits the guard on the LAKER move, he is to go opposite and set a screen for the forward. Diagram 8.6 shows this move. It is important to note that the forward running the UCLA move immediately gets back out of the lane if he doesn't IMMEDIATELY receive a pass from the post man.

A good, solid screen from the post man enables guard #1 to hit forward #4 for a quick lane jumper. If there is a defensive switch on this maneuver, then the post man executes a quick rear pivot, pins his man, and is prepared to receive a pass from #4.

If nothing is open yet, then the forward and post man continue to screen for each other. Eventually one of them will free himself for a quick lane jumper. See Diagram 8.7.

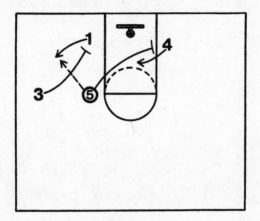

Diagram 8.6

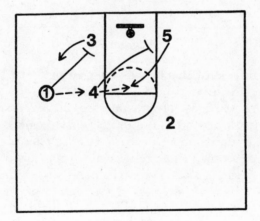

Diagram 8.7

Any time a pass is made to one of the frontliners cutting to the middle of the lane, another LAKER MOVE is executed by the passer. Diagram 8.7 shows #1 hitting #5 and then screening low for #3 on the baseline.

To complete the series, there must be some option should the strong side forward *not* be able to hit the post man to initiate the LAKER and UCLA moves. The post man is instructed to cut back door should his defensive man be in the passing lane, thereby cutting off the pass from #3 to the post man. If the back door cut is not open, then the post man simply executes the screen with the weak-side forward as described earlier. Diagram 8.8 shows these maneuvers. In such a move, the forward now becomes the post man and the post man will become the weak-side forward who will execute the next UCLA move. Thus, we have run the post man to his favorite spot on the court—the box—and given him a chance to power into the middle.

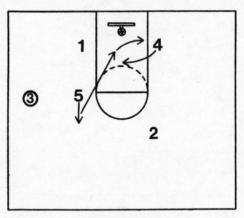

Diagram 8.8

Another possibility, should the post man be covered on the initial thrust, is to return the ball back to the point area—the top of the key. The guard and weak-side forward then execute a 2-on-2 maneuver. It is basically a free lance move—it could be a screen and roll, it could be a pass and cut thru option, it could be any type of improvisation. Diagram 8.9 shows the action between the point guard and weak-side forward. The diagram also shows what transpires on the other side of the court. As #3 releases his pass to the point, both he and the post man set a double screen on the baseline for guard #1. Thus another LAKER move, only this time off a double screen. Against certain teams, these latter moves described are the most effective of the entire sequence.

A final option should the post man not be able to get the pass to begin the UCLA and LAKER sequence is to rear screen for the post man and throw the ball over the top to the weak side. Diagram 8.10 shows this.

This rear screening action is always initiated by the weak-side forward who has an excellent view of the entire offense and defense. It is easy for this forward to simply come up behind the post man and call out his first name. Or, as another option, if the weak-side guard's man is sagging off to stop the play, a rear screen can be set for him. Diagram 8.11 shows this action, Again, it is keyed by the forward coming up behind and calling the guard's name.

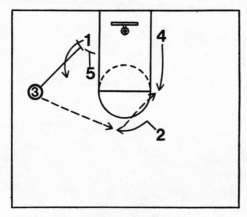

Diagram 8.9

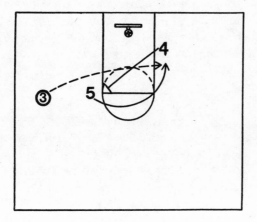

Diagram 8.10

There are several other options that can be employed in this series. What is most gratifying about this series is that the post man's talents—good passing or good 15 foot shooting or good screening or good power moves inside (or a combination of any of these) are utilized to the post man's advantage. Also, the pattern can be broken down easily for practice purposes. It is rather easy to set up a drill to work just on

LAKER MOVES 3-on-3. Also, a high-low situation, 2-on-2, working on the UCLA move, can be simulated in practice. The entire sequence can be

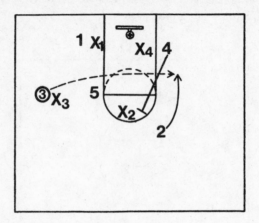

Diagram 8.11

broken down in this manner. This makes teaching rather simple. Because of the five basic options that the post man has when he receives the pass off the initial thrust, label this entire sequence the "5" SERIES. This makes it easy for the coach to signify it from the bench or for the captain to signal it from the floor by just raising a hand and spreading the five fingers.

LOW POST OFFENSE

In designing an offense to utilize a post man who is *not* a good passer or not a good 12-15 foot shooter but does operate rather well down low, stick with the same pattern as described earlier in this chapter but change the initial alignment. Start the post man at the low area and be set up in a 2-2-1 alignment as shown in Diagram 8.12.

The "5" series will now be run as before but with different players align-ments. Instead of the post man coming up high, the weak-side forward will. Instead of the strong guard cutting to the baseline, the weak-side guard will cut. The post man will simply go opposite the ball to the box area so that he can set up on the weak-side and be the UCLA man. Diagram 8.13 shows the basic movement.

The rest of the pattern remains the same. We have started out with a different initial alignment but gotten into the basic "5" series alignment

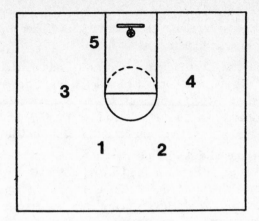

Diagram 8.12

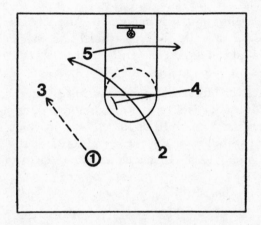

Diagram 8.13

after the first pass and first cuts. Thus, the LAKER, UCLA, and every other option is now available to be exploited. The main difference, though, is that the post man (a poor 15 foot shooter, a poor passer, but a good power man inside) is now the low post man weak-side running the UCLA moves.

QUICK SHOT OFFENSE

A well-prepared coach has his team ready to come from behind and play catch-up ball if the situation calls for this. Sometimes, it is difficult to make up ten or twelve points in several minutes with a set offense like the "5" series or even off a passing game or motion offense. Instead, an offense designed to get a quick shot within the matter of a few seconds is crucial to win several ball games.

In designing such an offense, simplicity and quickness of shot release are the two most important considerations. Once again decision time for the coach arises. Do you want to get your post man involved in the quick-shot offense? Or do you wish to keep the post man always near the board to get the offensive rebounds and second and third shots?

A situation that allows for both of these is a compromise answer to the question. A quick screen on the ball usually makes things happen. A shot, the screen and roll play, a defensive mistake on a switch—all of these are realistic possibilities when there is a screen on the ball. There is little denying that the screen on the ball in a situation when the team is trailing late in a ball game might result in some very poor shots being taken. But you can't score if you don't put the ball up there. And with time against you, it is important to try to create a quick shot —even though some of those quick shots might be poor ones. Especially if you do have a good, big post player, it is advantageous to get the ball up on the boards and let him go after it.

The simplest of quick shot offenses involves three basic concepts. *First,* using a 2-1-2 offensive set, the forwards can come up and screen for the guards as the center rolls opposite. This post man roll creates a screen and roll possibility for the guard and forward. If a shot is there, up it goes. Diagram 8.14 shows this move. If no shot is taken, then the rolling forward slides across the lane to screen the post man. All frontliners hit the boards.

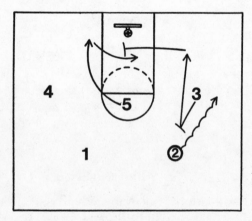

Diagram 8.14

Secondly, as soon as the ball is passed to the forward, the screen and roll maneuver will be executed with the post man as the screener. The screen can be made on either side of the forward—allowing him to go towards the baseline or towards the middle. Diagram 8.15 shows this. It is important that the other players stay clear of the side that the offense is operating on. If nothing develops from this, the rule remains constant: the man who screens and rolls then goes opposite to screen for the weak-side front-liner on that side.

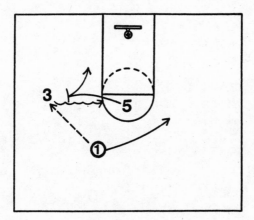

Diagram 8.15

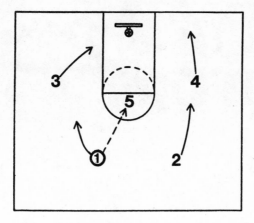

Diagram 8.16

The *third* option is to throw the ball to the high post man. He turns square up to the basket and either shoots the jumper or hits one of his teammates "filling" the open lanes to the basket. This is a good shot because of excellent movement to the boards by the other player. See Diagram 8.16.

This is the entire quick-shot offense. Simple rules and quick and easy shot opportunities utilize the post man in the roles you have determined best for him: as a rebounder, as a screener, as a passer.

9

SHUFFLING FOR THE
SMALL POST MAN

With a smaller post man or with a smaller, less talented team, a coach usually likes more control over his offense when they have to set up on a half court basis. The passing game or motion offense can be used effectively for a team with a small center, but others still want more control. Thus, in such a circumstance, a shuffle offense, with some passing game principles added, can prove highly beneficial and effective.

The shuffle offense can be so designed that it employs the patterned structure of a set offense and the freedom of the passing game. It allows the coach to run every player on his squad into the post area, thereby causing confusion on the part of the defense. Most coaches do not even teach their guards to defend in the post area. The shuffle will force your opponents to make some defensive adjustments and perhaps get away from their normal defensive game.

Conversely, the shuffle offense is more complex to teach because it demands that every single member of the squad be taught the principles of post play. This demands a lot of work and patience on the part of the coach. But generally speaking, all players like to post up at some time or other. All one has to do is go up in the gym or out to the playground and watch pick-up games to see how everyone likes to go "inside" the key to maneuver and shoot. You'd be surprised at the attention given to the coach when he is teaching the procedures and mechanics of posting up to players other than normal post men.

As mentioned previously in analyzing the small post player, one can use him in one of four ways: (1) use him at the high post; (2) let him "roam" inside or out; (3) play him like you would play a normal post in your normal offense; (4) rotate post men, and run different people in and out of the post area, thereby hoping to create confusion on the part of the defense.

If you opt for the last one, the shuffle offense best satisfies those goals. In analyzing the advantages of a shuffle offensive set and movement, one can readily see that it is a very simple pattern once the basic movement has been mastered. Also, you do get plenty of movement from this offense. Hence, the motion of a passing game and the pattern of a set offense is maintained in a type of coexistence.

Total team concepts are employed in the shuffle offense, something that is absolutely necessary for success if you don't have a good big man or good overall team talent. The very fact that each player plays each position all over the court is an advantage to a team without height. The revolving post men do pose defensive problems. Guards become forwards, forwards become post men, post men become wing or perimeter players.

Obviously, this system also has a great substitution advantage. You need not substitute by position (guard, forward, center). You can now substitute your sixth best player for whomever has to come out of the game. If the fast break isn't there, you can set up the shuffle pattern quite easily by simply filling five spots on the court with any man in any position. In general, the average-sized players are given a chance to use their normally superior quickness and agility, their cutting prowess and passing skills, and their intelligence in moving in and out of the post area in this particular offense.

THE SHUFFLE SET

The shuffle being talked about is no different from the traditional Drake or Auburn Shuffles. The numbering might be varied a little, but the basic patterns are the same.

Diagram 9.1 shows the traditional shuffle set. It is almost a 1-3-1 alignment, but for effectiveness, the #3 man should be a little higher than (not even with) the #5 man.

The players must master these positions, as the rotation will then be simple. Player #1 will go to #2's position, player #2 to #3's position, player #3 to #4's spot, player #4 to #5's position, and #5 will become the new #1 man.

Diagram 9.2 shows the traditional shuffle movement. Player #1 passes the ball to the weak-side wing man, #2. Player #3 makes a good angle cut off #5 (in the post area). Player #1 moves down the lane and #5 uses him as a picker and rubs off his rear, looking for a possible fifteen foot jumper. Player #1 continues down and screens for #4 who flashes across the lane high toward the ball.

Diagram 9.3 shows the new alignment if no one is open for the shot. Diagram 9.4 shows the rotation and how the new set or alignment is compared to the original set of Diagram 9.1. Whereas the strong side, as one looks at it, was on the left side in Diagram 9.1, the strong

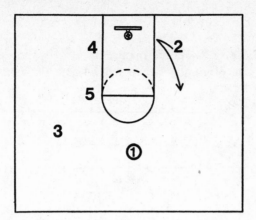

Diagram 9.1

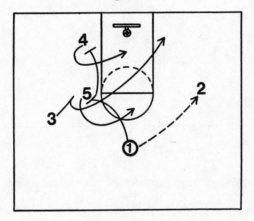

Diagram 9.2

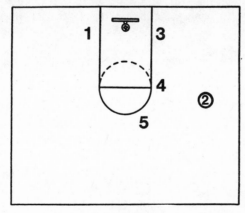

Diagram 9.3

side is now on the right side in Diagram 9.4. In other words, the offense has been "turned over." The #5 man becomes the new #1 man or point man. The original point man (#1) has become the new weak-side #2 man. The original #2 man has become the new #3 man (the cutter). The #4 man is the new #5 man, etc. As long as you can get the ball to the #2 man—the weak-side player—you can turn this over from side-to-side all day. Obviously, if you turn it over five times, all five men will have played all five positions.

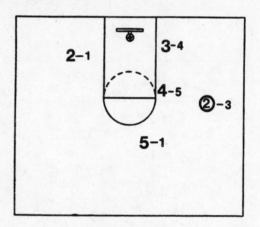

Diagram 9.4

The basic shots one would be looking for are these:

1. The #2 man for a quick 1-on-1 pop or dribble-drive shot.
2. The #3 man on the shuffle cut.
3. The #5 man coming off #1's screen for the jumper.
4. The #4 man bursting off #1's screen for the flash post shot.

TEACHING THE WEAK-SIDE SHUFFLE

There are a couple of secrets to be used in teaching the shuffle movement in practice sessions. First, use numbered cones and move them around the court for the players to learn the basic movements. Second, put the numbers 1 thru 5 on practice jerseys (using tape) and start in the original set as shown in Diagram 9.1 with the player at the point wearing jersey number 1, the weak-side wing man wearing jersey #2, and so on. Then move the players through the cuts and turn it over five different times, emphasizing to all squad members where each man—each number—is going.

It should be mentioned here that one of the best shots off the shuffle cut series is the quick jumper or drive for the #1 man. He initiates the sequence with a pass to the wing and cuts through, screening first for the #5 man and then the #4 man. On the "turn over," if he times the moves, the #1 man can pop out at the right time and momentarily free himself for the quick dribble-drive or shot. This is shown in Diagram 9.5.

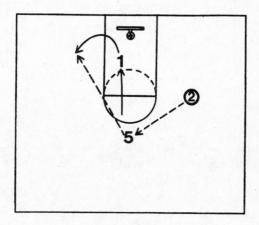

Diagram 9.5

The basic shuffle movement is initiated by a pass to the #2 man—the weak-side wing. Good defensive teams try to shut down the entire shuffle series by really playing the #2 man tough and not allowing him to receive the ball. ALL team members must be well-schooled in the skill of getting open and running the backdoor cut.

THE STRONG-SIDE GAME

Because of the constant overplay of the #2 man, it is necessary to combine a very good strong-side game into the basic shuffle pattern. In many instances, the strong-side game is more effective than the weak-side game. After an initial shuffle cut off the weak-side and a rotation of the post player, get quickly into the strong-side game and really rattle the defense. The strong-side terminology is very consistent with other offensive moves mentioned earlier in the book. A LAKER MOVE is a baseline screen. A UCLA MOVE is a high-low post move. A SPLIT is a cutting or scissoring action off the post. A "2" MOVE is any type of clear out. And "MOTION" refers to anything else. A pass to the #3 man initiates the strong-side action. See Diagram 9.6.

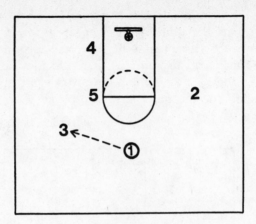

Diagram 9.6

Once #3 has received the ball, he has a variety of options open to him. He may hit the post man and go screen on the baseline for #4— a LAKER MOVE. While this is happening, #2 takes his man low and runs a quick UCLA into the middle, while point man #1 FLARES. Diagram 9.7 shows this movement. The UCLA movement as initiated by #2 is further explained in Diagram 9.8.

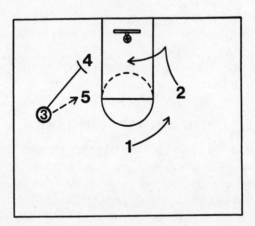

Diagram 9.7

After hitting the post, should #3 move toward the point, then he is running a split or scissors with #1. The low baseline man must clear the area, as depicted in Diagram 9.9.

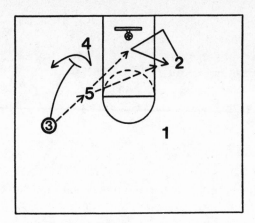

Diagram 9.8

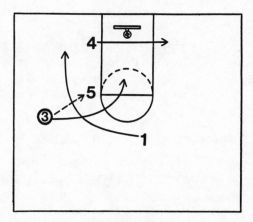

Diagram 9.9

A sound basic rule for any offense is to clear out if the dribbler begins to dribble at you. This enables the ball-handler to have a one-on-one opportunity. So if the #3 man starts bouncing the ball, #4 and #5 clear out of his way. If nothing develops, they should follow simple motion or passing game rules.

MOTION AND PASSING

For a coach who likes to employ motion or passing game principles, the shuffle lends itself to that effectively. After a few patterned cuts off the weak-side #2 man, a quick pop to the strong side lend itself to motion principles. This is often very effective against a good defensive club, as they get themselves set for the patterned stuff and are not as readily adaptable to passing game cuts or movements.

In many ways it is wise to enter a game with this type of game plan: Much like a football team wants to establish its ground or running game so that it can eventually take to the air, you may want to establish your weak-side regular shuffle cut offense so that the defense begins to overplay and anticipate them. While the defense is looking for the shuffle series weak side, hit them quickly with the strong-side material—LAKERS, UCLA's SPLITS and other passing and motion game options.

It should be obvious that a mastery of the regular shuffle rotation is necessary to make all of this go, but a basic rule to follow is this: IF there is some deviation in any manner from the shuffle cuts, then immediately follow motion or passing game rules.

Now go back to the original reason for this offense—for this chapter. If you do not have a good, big post player and want to revolve men into the post area, you can see that this offense accomplishes that rather effectively. There is constant movement—some patterned and set, others free-lance and motioned. There is constant interchange of post players—taking advantage of the quickness and mobility necessary to play this offense. And there is a lot of emphasis on TEAM play— an emphasis that is necessary for a small team with a small post man.

PREPARING FOR THE SHUFFLE

Chapter 2 described several pre-season and off-season programs designed to prepare the post player for his season. The weight-training, stretching, and exercise programs described therein would be beneficial for the post player no matter what offense he were placed in. However, because the shuffle offense does not really involve a set post player but instead rotates post players and sends a normal post player to different positions on the court—both inside and outside—there is a little different philosophy on preparing players during the off-season and pre-season to play such an offense. Instead of emphasizing the power moves and power shooting inside, now one must stress ball-handling, shooting both from the inside and perimeter, cutting, shooting off the dribble. Thus, when we have decided to use the shuffle offense for a given season, our players are given a program to work on over the summer months that will best prepare them for this offense. Realizing that many players will have to work during the off-season, the program is designed for one person but can be adapted to two or more. Realizing again that the shuffle offense forces each player to play the post at some time or another during the sequence, this program for the post player really becomes a program for *all* players.

The emphasis in this program is offense: dribbling, shooting, power game inside, and movement without the basketball. The program is designed to run for about one hour, with the shooting part of it to occupy the major portion of that time. The program is also a good conditioner and can be used in its entirety or in part for a normal practice session during the regular season.

All that is needed for the program is a basketball, a goal, a clock, and a jump rope. Enthusiasm and a desire to improve one's game are the necessary inner tools needed by the player to complete the program. The players are instructed to do the program at least three days a week during the off-season, five days if they so desire. As in the programs described in Chapter 2, all players are instructed to take the week-ends off from basketball and all basketball related activities.

Since the shuffle does have opportunities for a quick one-on-one move and since all players will move to spots along the perimeter of the court, it is important that all players be able to go with or dribble the basketball. Whereas in other offenses the post player may take one dribble at the most along the lane, now in this offense he may be required to go more than that.

Dribbling Work

All dribble drills are begun at mid-court or its equivalent on an outside basket. The player will dribble down one side of the court and shoot a layup, dribble directly out to the 10 second line (or its equivalent), and then dribble in the other side, using the other hand. Diagram 9.10 shows this basic movement.

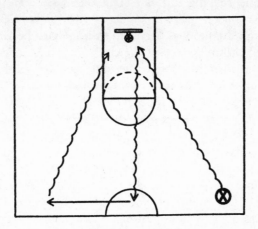

Diagram 9.10

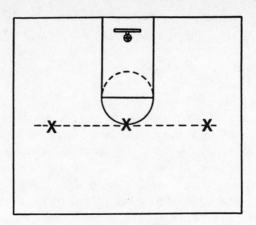

Diagram 9.11

The player will work on four dribble moves: the on-side dribble, the change of pace dribble, the cross-over dribble (or its equivalent), and the reverse spin dribble. He will work on each one of these for two minutes each, switching hands as he switches sides of the court. The move will be executed at the top of the circle (key) or at an imaginary line drawn across the top of the circle from sideline to sideline. So, three times the move will be made. Diagram 9.11 illustrates this point, and the three points of execution are marked with an X on the diagram.

The player starts on the right side of the ten-second line and begins a high speed dribble toward the basket. When he reaches the tip of the circle extended (marked by an "X" on Diagram 9.11) he executes an on-side move—faking with his head, shoulders, and legs to the left while keeping the ball at his right side. He then drives to the basket and shoots the right-handed layup. He retrieves the ball as it comes through the net and begins to dribble out toward the 10 second line. When he reaches the top of the circle, he again executes an on-side move. When he then hits the ten-second line, he dribbles parallel to the left side of the court from which spot he drives to the hoop, stopping at the top of the circle extended (marked again by an "X" on Diagram 9.11) and executing an on-side move. After driving in from the left side and shooting a left-handed layup, he repeats this same procedure for the remaining two minutes. At the end of the two minute period, he then begins to work on the change of pace dribble. After two minutes of this, he goes to the cross-over dribble or its equivalent. By a cross-over equivalent, we mean behind-the-back or between-the-legs dribble. The player is free to choose to master any one or all of these. And finally, he works on the reverse spin dribble.

After eight minutes of dribble work are up, the player will grab his rope and jump continuously for two minutes, trying for quickness. After completing this task, he may rest for two minutes.

Shooting Work

The next phase of the program is the shooting part. Competitiveness and concentration are so important in this phase. Too often players work on their shooting in a rather haphazard fashion. They grab the ball and fire a twenty footer, go get it and shoot a layup, amble out to the top of the circle and fire one from there, and so on. This accomplishes little; in fact, it probably breeds some bad habits. Every time our players work alone on shooting, we encourage them to "battle a pro." Make believe that you are going up against a professional star. You score two points for every shot that you make, while the pro gets two points for every shot that you miss.

At the same time, don't just shoot at random. Pick out five spots on the court where the team offense will get the player his shot. In the case of the shuffle offense, there are five logical spots from which the shot most likely will occur. Since all players will ultimately move to each of these spots, the players must practice from all of them. The five spots from which the shot most likely will come off the WEAK SIDE movement are indicated with an X in Diagram 9.12. Spot #1 is the wing player and the shot off the initial pass. Spots #2 and #3 are shots that the cutter will normally get. Spot #4 is the flash post shot. Spot #5 post man coming off the cutter to reverse the ball, Diagram 9.13 shows the strong side shot opportunities usually afforded by the shuffle. Spot #1 is the Laker Shot. Spot #2 is the UCLA move. Spot #3 is the wing shot. Spot

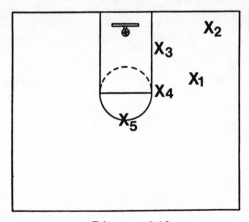

Diagram 9.12

#4 is the high post shot when the defense sags. And Spot #5 is the guard flaring to the open area.

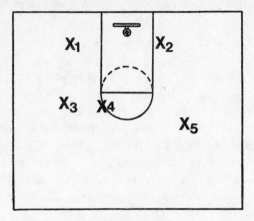

Diagram 9.13

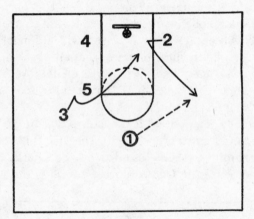

Diagram 9.14

The procedure that the player is instructed to work on from these spots is this: He will shoot five shots from each spot. He will shoot these from a stand, pretending that he has just received a pass. (He can even simulate the pass by flipping the ball up in the air with backspin and catching it). After having shot five from each spot for a total of twenty-five shots (he also keeps track of the score as he is battling a pro star), he will shoot five more from each spot, only this time he will take one dribble to that spot. Hence, another total of twenty-five shots will have been taken. Next, he will take two dribbles to get to his spot. So twenty-five more shots have been taken. And finally, he will shoot five more from each spot, using whatever procedure he wants

—stand, three dribbles, behind-the-back move, anything the player wants.

Upon completion of this work, the player has a total of 100 shots— twenty from each of five spots along the court. At the same time, he has been shooting against a pro star, giving himself two points for every made shot and the pro two points for every missed shot. The final total—score of the player and the pro combined—will equal 200. It would be helpful if the player could record his shooting stats and bring them in to the coach when the school term starts. Following this, the player will jump rope for two minutes and then take a two minute rest before beginning the next phase.

Inside Game Work

Since every player on the squad will be a post player in the shuffle offense, it is mandatory that all know how to take the ball up tough inside the key. Therefore, as a part of the off-season program for the SHUFFLE team, the next phase deals with the offensive re- bounding drills described previously in Chapter 6. A quick summary of those drills are: rebounding both sides of the boards, tipping right and left, race and tip, rip and power, rip-fake-power, rip and step under, rip-fake and step under, rip and hook, the hand toughener, the two ball dunks, and the super slam—the latter three are for only those who can hit the rim and dunk. This entire sequence can be accomplished—after a few trials—in about 12 minutes. Upon completion of this, the player jumps rope for two minutes and takes a two minute rest.

Movement Without the Ball

The final phase of the program is movement without the basketball. This is so important to any offense that it is often amazing how many coaches neglect work in this area. Particularly in the shuffle, the #2 man must be adept at getting himself open and the #3 man must be equally adept at freeing himself off the cut. Diagram 9.14 will refresh your memory on these movements.

There are three basic moves and cuts to be worked on. Each coach will probably have a different term or phrase to describe them. But, in this work, we will use the terms employed by our staff. The three moves or cuts are: THE NORMAL CUT, THE "L" MOVE, AND THE DIP. Diagram 9.15 shows the normal cut; Diagram 9.16, the "L" move; and Diagram 9.17, the dip.

Each move is to be worked on for two minutes. If working alone, the player must concentrate on good fakes, good footwork, and good angles. It becomes easier if someone will pass the ball to the player as he pops out on the move. If working alone, it is best for the player to simply lay the basketball down at the spot where he wishes to receive the ball, make his move to that spot, pick the ball up, and then go with it. The latter point is important: the player is always to do something with the ball after he receives it (or picks it off the ground). He may dribble drive to the hoop or shoot the jumper. After working on each of these moves for two minutes, the player jumps rope for two more minutes and if time remains in his hour, he shoots free throws. This completes the program.

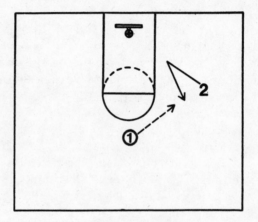

Diagram 9.15

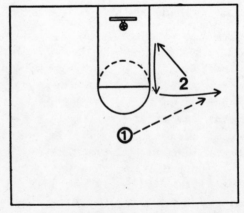

Diagram 9.16

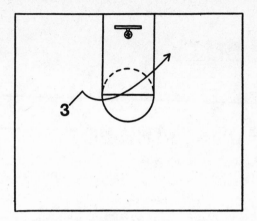

Diagram 9.17

Though this specific program was designed to help players ac-
climate themselves to the shuffle offense, we have found that it can
benefit any player working in any type of offense. The coach should
simply revise the shooting spots, depending upon where he desires
his players to shoot from. Otherwise, the program can remain as is.
Most offenses do demand good ball-handling and driving skills to
the basket, good inside game, and finally movement without the ball.
Therefore, this program of self-improvement can be a benefit to anyone
who hopes to improve his game.

10

REVOLVING A ZONE OFFENSE
AROUND THE POST

Zone defenses are becoming more and more popular at all levels of basketball. It is increasingly important for the coach to have developed a zone offense to combat the various types of zone defenses thrown at a team during a given season. It is better to run one offense well than several offenses poorly.

Philosophically speaking, every coach must know what he wants to do against a zone and he must communicate this to his players. The basic way to beat the zone is to TILT THE ZONE TO ONE SIDE, MAKE IT FLOW, MOVE, AND THEN COUNTER IT QUICKLY TO THE OTHER SIDE. Therefore, everyone on the team must visualize the phrase: TILT, FLOW, AND COUNTER. It is the fundamental way to smash zone defenses.

Once again, the post man becomes the key to COUNTERING a zone defense. He either is a decoy coming to the ball, suckering the defense in, or he is the man countering the zone with quick passes to the weak side from the strong side.

Because, as often stated in this book, there are various kinds and sizes of post players, it is important to develop an offense that can use any type of post player with just minor adjustments to the basic structure of the offense. This was what was done in Chapter 8 against a man defense in developing a man-to-man offense. A 1-2-2, double low post offense, against the zone, has been a very effective set from which to attack any zone. The set can use two big men at the low post, or two small men, or one of each. The options off such a set are many and varied and obviously very hard to defense.

1-2-2 POWER OFFENSE

Before explaining the basic movement of the 1-2-2 zone offense, it is necessary to go over some basic principles of zone attack. Since most teams are right-handed and will attack right most of the time, start the post man you want to get the ball to on the opposite or left block. It is much more difficult to defend a post man flashing to the ball. Post men should be schooled in coming to open gaps in the zone to receive the ball. They should realize that if they start behind the back line of the zone (which the 1-2-2 zone set enables them to do against any type of zone defense) they can "lose themselves" from the zone and flash to open gaps much easier. Don't be stereotyped; vary the move. Also, the arms-up target technique is to be employed at all times. Being a threat is half of the battle in successfully attacking and defeating zone defenses. Cutters going through the zone should be used by the post man as a type of moving screen. Zone defenses have a difficult time defending against the screen, especially a moving screen. Post men should also be ready to step off the lane out on the baseline to get the ball. Chesting the ball after reception is a necessary skill that was talked about earlier. And the post man should always think PASS if the shot isn't there. Remember, he is in a position to COUNTER the zone with a weak-side pass. Such a pass often results in the un-contested 12-15 foot jumper that just breaks the back of zone defenses. Not moving fast, but moving QUICKLY and reading the defense are two skills that a post man needs no matter what the defense is set up in. These are just a few of the general principles that the post man must keep in mind when playing against zone defenses.

In the 1-2-2 set, court positioning in the initial alignment is crucial to success. At least one of the two low men should be behind the back line of the zone. This means that if one of them has to start on the end line, almost on the base line out of bounds, that is fine. As long as the defense has to turn its head to find the offensive low man, the purpose has been served. Remember that zones can be beaten in a quick flash if one of the defenders turns his head to the ball.

The two wing men should line themselves up at or above the free throw line extended. They should not start below the free throw line. The point man must be adept at dribble penetrating from the top of the circle. All team members must understand that they must shorten all passing lanes in attacking the zone defense. Sometimes a short, quick dribble from the point area best accomplishes this. They should also realize that diagonal passes and skip passes (passes where the next logical receiver is skipped and the ball thrown to the second most logical receiver) just kill a zone. This initial alignment is shown in Diagram 10.1.

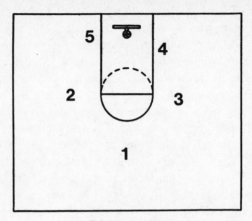

Diagram 10.1

Perhaps the biggest secret of this alignment is to show the weaker of the two post men in the initial alignment (#4) by starting him above the box and in the middle of the zone, while the other post man starts behind the back line of the zone and tries to "hide himself" down there.

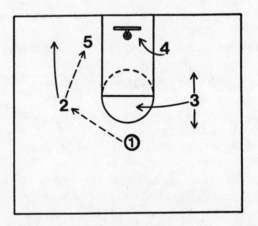

Diagram 10.2

Before putting in any set moves off the 1-2-2 zone attack, remind everyone that any time a post man is open, the ball is to go inside to him. This could occur when the ball is at the wing area as shown in Diagram 10.2 or from the point as shown in Diagram 10.3.

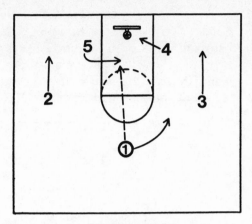

Diagram 10.3

In both diagrams, notice what the "other" post man does when his buddy receives the ball—he loops to the basket. This "buddy system" —post man looking for his fellow post man—is quite an effective move. Notice also the movement of the wing men—they "fill" open slots in the zone defense. Realize that when the ball has gone inside, you have tilted the zone and made it move. If the post man doesn't have the shot, several passing lanes are open to him—lanes that counter the defense and lead to an open 12-15 foot jumper. Diagram 10.4 shows several of these lanes when the ball has been placed inside from the left wing.

The basic play off the 1-2-2 zone offense is the CUT THROUGH. This move gives the zone defense everything that it doesn't want to see:

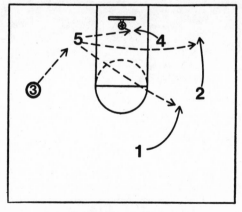

Diagram 10.4

cutters going through post area, screens, weak-side countering action, and quick ball movement. The play starts with the ball put to either wing area. If the low post man is not open he quickly pops out along the baseline, looking for a quick, short baseline jumper. See Diagram 10.5.

The wing who hits the baseline man executes a quick cut—a give and go type cut—through the defense. If open, he is to be given the ball.

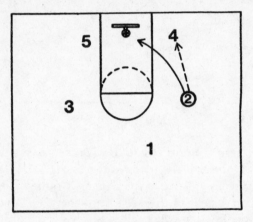

Diagram 10.5

As soon as the cutter has gone through, the two other perimeter people (#1 and #3) rotate to fill the vacated spots. #1 fills #2's spot on the wing, while #3 fills the point area vacated by #1. The ball is quickly reversed from the baseline to the wing to the point and the point man looks for cutter #2 who is coming around the low post man's (#5's) screen. Diagram 10.6 shows this basic movement.

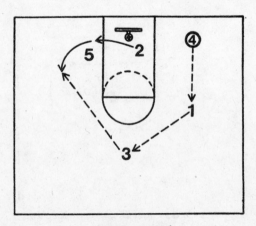

Diagram 10.6

The zone defense has been tilted to the right side; now it is caught moving quickly to the left. The back man of the zone defense is the man to be screened by the low post man. If the defender gets caught in the screen, then the original cutter, #2, should be open. If the defender tries to play the cutter and gets through the screen, then the low post man simply moves up the lane for the ball from the point. See Diagram 10.7.

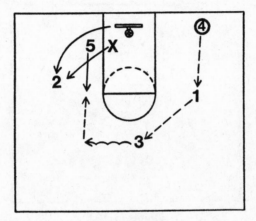

Diagram 10.7

Thus far, the zone has been tilted and moved. However, even though this cut through action results in many shots, maybe the best move off the series is the COUNTERING ACTION initiated by the low pass man to whom the initial play was run. After #4 releases his pass to the wing, he hesitates for a count and then starts a SLIDE towards the lane and the circle therein. Diagram 10.8 shows this movement.

Many times, especially after running the cutter through and hitting him a couple of times, #4 is open for a direct pass from the point man. As the low post man #4 vacates the area, the wing man fills it. This creates an excellent alignment from which to counter the zone which is moving, trying to follow the ball and overplaying the cutter coming off the opposite low post man.

Diagram 10.9 shows the low post man dumping the ball off to #1 on a back door type move. Or, a direct pass from the point man (#3) over the top to #1 can result in a lot of uncontested jump shots of the 10-12 foot variety. The zone defense has a very difficult time stopping this movement. Especially if the offense will throw a skip pass or two on the initial cut through does it make it doubly tough to cover. For example, instead of passing the ball from the baseline to wing to point to cutter coming off the baseline screen, (shown in Diagram 10.6), the ball can be passed directly from the wing to the cutter, by-passing the point man. The defense now is really perplexed as to what move to stop. Remember, good zones move and react quickly on the ball. So by getting the ball and players moved to one side and quickly countering the opposite, zone defenses can be run ragged.

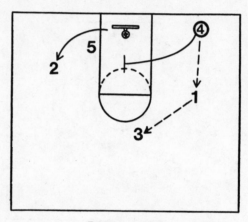

Diagram 10.8

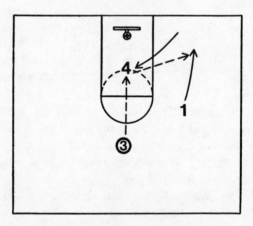

Diagram 10.9

Based upon the premise that defenses will soon begin to play the play after being burned several times, an effective option off the CUT THROUGH is "S"—which stands for "SCREEN." The movement is exactly the same as that of the CUT THROUGH except that now the cutter does not cut all the way around and through the defense. He alters his route to that shown in Diagram 10.10 in order to set a rear or blind side screen for the point man.

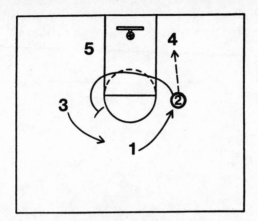

Diagram 10.10

When the ball is now returned to the point man via the wing, the point dribble-drives off the screen. Diagram 10.11 shows the pressure that this move exerts on the back line men of the zone defense. Should the back man of the zone come up to play the driver (in which case, the low post man can simply pop out along the baseline for a baby jumper) or should the back stay back and allow the dribbler the 12-15 foot jumper? Diagram 10.11 shows the dilemma.

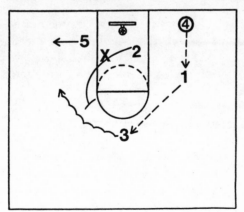

Diagram 10.11

No matter what zone defensive alignment is being employed, the CUT THROUGH SERIES is a major problem for the defense. Add to this another set play option which is called STOP. It is nothing more than a LAKER move—a baseline screen. The cutter fakes as if he were going through to the opposite side, but, after getting to the middle of the lane and allowing the ball to be returned to the wing and faked to the point, comes back off the low post screen. Diagram 10.12 explains the action.

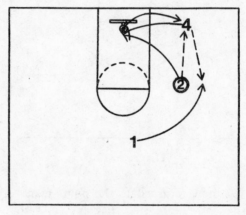

Diagram 10.12

#1, now at the wing, looks toward the point as if the ball were being moved around, while #4—the low post man—steps inside to screen for wing man #2—the cutter. This variation adds a new dimension to the entire series.

The post man's importance in this sequence is central to the success of the pattern. No matter whether he is the low post man on strong side who receives the initial pass and slides toward the middle, or the low post man on the weak side who sets the screen on the CUT THROUGH, the post man's moves are crucial to success. He must be a screener, a low post power player, a decoy, a man who slides from the baseline to the middle to shoot a turn around lane jumper, a passer, a reader of defenses. His movement—his cuts and slides—must be timed to perfection and must be executed properly. For instance, he must pop out along the baseline at the right moment to free himself for that short jumper or the pass to initiate the CUT THROUGH motion. He must slide—with a defensive slide step and arms raised—into the middle on the reverse of the ball, so that, if nothing else, he acts as a decoy suckering the defense with him. He must not go too soon on this move. And he must give a good target. Diagram 10.13 reviews this particular move.

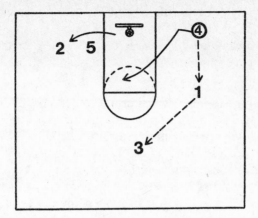

Diagram 10.13

Should the point guard be unable to get the ball to the wing on perimeter, immediately go into a high post series. Both low men come flashing up the free throw lane to the free throw line extended. The point guard whips the ball to one of them, while the other angles down the lane for a possible return pass. The other players simply fill the open spots as indicated in Diagram 10.14.

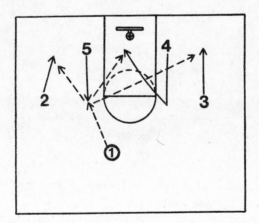

Diagram 10.14

The diagram shows the possible passing options of the post man. If the post man is a good jump shooter, allow him to take this shot, as excellent board play results from the cuts of the other players. Timing is essential to execute this "8" series. But above all, the key is recognition by the post man that he is needed to open a passing lane, since the two

perimeter wing men are being overplayed. After passing the ball off
to either wing man, the post man should follow his shot for a possible
return pass. In Diagram 10.14, if the post man hit #3 roving to the baseline, then the post man should immediately flash across the lane, arms
up, for the return pass or a good rebounding slot.

A good overload play is important to a zone offense because it
overshifts the defense to one side and enables the offense to counter
the other more quickly. In running an overload off a 1-2-2 set, pass the
ball to a wing and run the opposite low man across the baseline off his
buddy's (other low man's) screen. It is important to keep the wing man
at least at the free throw line extended and not below. If below, it tends
to jam up the series. If the post man is open and is a good baseline jump
shooter, he is to take the shot. If the defense rushes out on him, he can
dump it inside to his "buddy." Diagram 10.15 shows this.

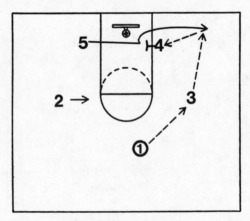

Diagram 10.15

Remember that diagonal passes and skip passes hurt the zone
defense. See in Diagram 10.15 how #5 can throw a quick diagonal to
#2 who has stepped to the free throw line extended. Most zone defenses
are very vulnerable to this particular diagonal pass. Continuing with
the OVERLOAD sequence, if the post man doesn't have the shot, he
returns the ball to the wing who returns it to the point. Now comes the
most effective move of the entire sequence. After the wing returns the
ball to the point he initiates a cut through to the opposite side. However,
his cut is somewhat slow—not quick. The reason for this is that the
post man is going to come right off the rear end of the cutter towards

the middle of the lane at the circle. Generally, he will be open off this moving type of screen. See Diagram 10.16.

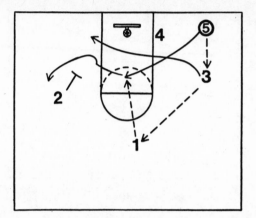

Diagram 10.16

Once the ball has been passed into the multi-purpose area—the key —the zone is at the mercy of the offense. Post man #5 can shoot the jumper with good board positioning by his teammates. He can pass to his buddy #4 for a power move. Or he can whip the ball to perimeter player #2. If the pass cannot be made to the post man, he continues his slide across the lane where perimeter player #2 picks the back man of the zone. Now remember that the zone has been tilted to one side—the overload side. The quick ball movement has the zone moving quickly and rather blindly. It is very easy for the defense to be picked or screened.

Diagram 10.16 shows #2's pick and how #5 uses this. If #5 is a good jump shooter, then he has a good shot. If not, cutter #3 has posted up low or the ball can be returned to the point man. If the pass is not made from the point to the middle, then the point man takes one quick dribble-drive back towards the original overload side and looks for post man #4 who is posting up on the defense. This move quickly counters the flow of the zone. Diagram 10.17 shows this move.

This OVERLOAD gives a good jump-shooting post man several opportunities to score from 12-15 foot range. It also creates a definite distraction for the defense as he slides up and through the multi-purpose area, suckering the zone in and creating other passing routes. It can be run towards either side and often works best when the poorer shooting post man is the overload man and is used as a decoy so that the ball can be eventually thrown inside on the reverse to the other post player.

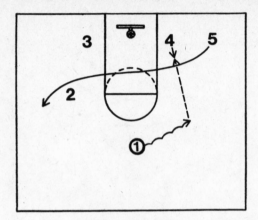

Diagram 10.17

1-3-1 HI/LOW POST OFFENSE

Against some tough defensive teams, it may be necessary to start a post man at the high post in order to prevent the overplay of the wings. This maneuver, with an offensive man stationed at the high post and hence in the middle of the zone defense, causes the defense to collapse around him, thus freeing the wings. Should the defense align themselves to match up with the offense in a 1-3-1 set, then two guards could dribble the ball up, and one of them can dribble the ball to the wing area from which the offense can be initiated.

The 1-3-1 zone offense is the same as the 1-2-2 zone offense in all aspects but ONE: the initial alignment is different. The different look that this set gives the defense is often enough to confuse them or make them think that the offense is changing its basic attack of the zone. However, if the ball is passed to a wing, then the high post can do one of two things. First, he can roll opposite the pass, while his "buddy," the low post man, always goes to the ball side. Second, he can roll to the strong side, while the low post man fades to the weak side. Either way, a 1-2-2 offensive set has been achieved and the team is now ready to run its normal zone offense: CUT THROUGHS, 8-series, or OVERLOAD. If a pass is made directly to the high post player at the free throw line, the low post man loops into the middle while the three perimeter players fill open slots. See Diagram 10.18. Needless to say, a well-drilled post man will immediately, after reception, pivot and face the basket. He is now a triple-threat.

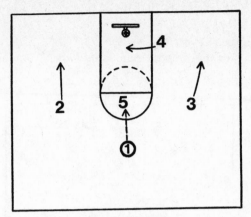

Diagram 10.18

The advantage of this 1-3-1 offensive set against the zone is its simplicity. One zone offense to attack all zone defenses. Different looks to the defense without changing the basic offense allows the coach more freedom, time, and flexibility to teach more individual skills and techniques.

SET PLAYS VERSUS THE ZONE

To be completely thorough and totally prepared, a coach should have his team ready to get one shot in a crucial situation against a zone defensive team. That shot may be a last second shot of a game or a quarter, or could be one that is necessary to change the momentum after a time out.

There are certain characteristics that this set play should take on, if, as indicated in the previous paragraph, it is planned for use in a special situation. First, the play should be rather basic. The coach should spend most of his practice time on fundamentals and the basic offensive patterns. The set plays should have a minimum of passing and dribbling in order to cut down on possible errors. Secondly, the shot should come off the set play rather quickly. Thirdly, rebound position should be guaranteed from the shot.

The 1-2-2 set is again used as the base for operation of the set plays against the zone defense. A very simple play that is designed to get a 15-17 foot jumper or a quick jam inside to a post man is the "TOP" play. The ball is passed from the point to the wing and quickly returned to the point again. The point man then goes to the opposite wing, causing the zone to tilt and flow to that side. When the opposite wing has the ball he looks across court and fires a cross-court top pass to the other wing who has slipped down behind the defense. The low post man on his side screens the deepest man in the zone. The wing has the jumper or a quick pass to the low post man should the defender come rushing out. Diagram 10.19 shows the play.

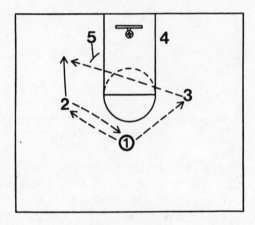

Diagram 10.19

In years gone by, coaches tended to discourage this cross court pass. But nowadays with the quickness and agility that players possess, it has become a fundamental pass in the game—especially effective against the zone defense.

As indicated in the overload move, a moving screen is very difficult to defend, especially by a zone defense. Though the legality of such a move is often questioned on paper, there is little doubt that such a move is easy to get away with under game conditions. Officials rarely call this so-called violation. The "2" move begins with the point man dribbling the ball at the wing man. The wing man fakes out, as if to receive a pass, then cuts through the lane to screen for the opposite low man. Meanwhile, the strong-side low man pops out five or six feet along the baseline, forcing a defender to cover him. The low post man on the opposite side runs right by and off the moving screen set by the wing who has cut through. A quick pass from the point to the post man results in a quick lane jumper. Diagram 10.20 shows this move.

Wing man #3 has to be very conscious and aware of whom to screen. He is not just running to a spot, he is actually picking out the defender most likely to cover the flashing low post man #5. For example, in a 2-1-2 zone, it most likely would be the middle man. In a 1-2-2 zone, it would be one of the low men, particularly the weak-side low man.

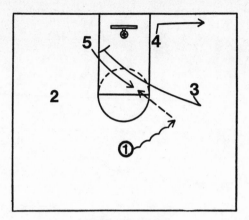

Diagram 10.20

Intelligent reading of the defense is a must to screen the zone and attack it successfully.

A final set play combines the screening movement, the cross-court pass, and some cutting. It is very similar to the TOP except that now the point man, after hitting the wing, cuts to the opposite wing who, in turn, fills the point area. In other words, the three perimeter players will pass and cut away and fill for each other. The wing man with the ball is always looking over-the-top for the cross-court pass to the opposite wing who has sneaked down off the low post man's screen. This action is explained in Diagrams 10.21 and 10.22.

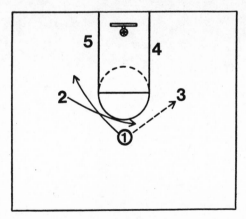

Diagram 10.21

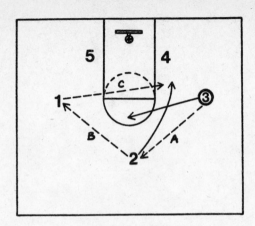

Diagram 10.22

While all of this perimeter action is taking place, the post man must pose a definite threat inside. He utilizes all his skills and movements that have been taught to him: posting up principles, proper target, finding the open gaps in the zone, and the like. An effective zone offense must revolve around the post man—whether he be the one getting the ball or just acting as a decoy. The post man.is the hub of the team, and this is no more vividly shown than in the 1-2-2 zone offense.

11

POST PLAY IN THE PASSING GAME

POST RULES VS. MAN DEFENSE

If the coach decides to use a motion or passing game offense, then he has some major decisions to make again on how to use the post man. The first question revolves around the number of post men to be employed. Shall one post man be used? Two? Or perhaps an open post with everyone having an option of roaming into the multi-purpose area? Second, how should the post men be used? Should they be employed primarily as screeners? As rebounders? As scorers? As passers? Or a combination of any or all of these?

A motion or passing game is an offense based on recognizing what the defense is doing and where and how its men are playing. It is based on constant movement by all five players to positions on the court that develop because of the defensive play. Instead of set patterns or plays being followed (patterns or plays that are often run regardless of what the defense is doing), concepts and rules are taught and the players adjust to the defense and use the rules accordingly.

The passing game or motion offense has numerous advantages over the set or patterned offense. All five people are in motion. This gives the defense all kinds of problems. Such an offense emphasizes the basics of the game: passing, cutting, screening. The offense teaches concentration as each player has to watch and observe where teammates are moving to. The passing game is difficult to scout and very difficult for the defense to anticipate. Freedom for the players is another advantage of the offense. It is simple and can be run off a multiplicity of sets. And the team using this offense can play any-sized players. You don't need to play players by positions: two guards, two forwards, and a post man.

Such an offense poses some difficulties also. The coach does not have a predetermined sequence of movement to follow as play develops. The passing game is susceptible to the fast break, and rebounding could be a problem in such an offense. Confusion could reign until the prin-

ciples are fully grasped. And the coach is not assured of good floor
balance at all times.

Most passing game offenses have similar rules, though each coach
usually adds one or two of his own that are different from the norm.
Remember, the more rules and restrictions placed on the players, the
more the offense is becoming patterned.

Basic rules for the perimeter players in a motion or passing game
offense include the following:

1. Don't make two consecutive cuts into the same area of the court.
2. All cuts are to be good, angle cuts.
3. Basic cuts to be employed are:
    —cut inside the ball.
    —cut away from the ball.
    —fill cut—filling an open slot on the court.
    —replace cut—where a player fakes as if he were going away
      but comes back to the original spot.
4. The man with the ball must square up and face the basket for
   a count of two.
5. The best screen is one for a teammate below you on the court—
   in other words, a down screen. Horizontal and back screens are
   also useful.
6. If dribbled at by a teammate, clear the area.
7. If a teammate ball fakes at you, clear the area.

The rules for the post man (or men) include the following:

1. Post players will be designated—one, two, or open post.
2. If the post man doesn't get the ball by a count of "2", he goes
   low, goes opposite, or replaces himself (fakes opposite but
   comes back).
3. Post man should think screen.
4. High post best options are to roll ball side or screen down.
5. Low post best options are to start opposite and come to the
   ball or back or rear screen.

In dealing with the post man in such an offense, the coach must
emphasize passing and cutting fundamentals. Drills on these have been
mentioned in previous chapters. However, a third fundamental that is
instrumental to the passing game is SCREENING. The post player, since
he is in the multi-purpose area of the court, becomes the chief screener
in this offense. He must be able to down screen, screen away, cross
screen, and rear or back screen. He must be schooled in the techniques
of all of these.

Because the post man is so crucial and necessary to any good offense, the coach can ill afford to lose him on fouls—particularly silly offensive fouls. Therefore, it is important to go over proper screening techniques with all players, but especially the post man. He should be taught all screens are to be set stationary with a good, wide base—feet spread shoulder's width apart. If the defensive player being screened is within the line of vision of the screener, then the screener can get as close as possible to the man being screened *without making contact*. If the screener is setting a pick on a man who has his back to the screener— in other words, the man being screened cannot see the screener within his normal line of vision—then the screen must be set in such a manner that the man being screened is allowed one normal step before contact with the screen. Understanding of these screening rules will prevent a lot of useless offensive fouls on the post man.

Another screening principle that must be emphasized is this: when the defense switches to play the cutter, then the post man or screener should immediately go to the ball. He must be taught the proper pivot to make so that he pins the defense behind him. If executed correctly, the screener comes to the ball with the defense pinned behind him. An example of such a maneuver is shown in Diagram 11.1.

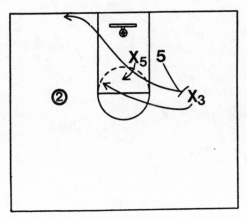

Diagram 11.1

In the diagram, the post man sets a rear or back pick for teammate #3. The defense switches as #3 cuts toward the baseline. The post man should then execute a reverse pivot, pinning his back to the defensive man. He then comes directly towards #2 who has the ball. If executed properly, the defender will trail #5 across the lane.

A single post man in the passing game will most often roll toward the ball or go screen opposite. These two moves are shown in Diagrams 11.2 and 11.3.

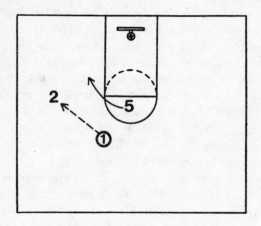

Diagram 11.2

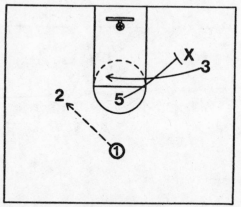

Diagram 11.3

If the post man is to be used primarily as a scorer, then he must be taught how to *use* a screen. Other squad members must be constantly looking for the post man in order to free him for a quick jumper. The technique of recognizing how the defense is playing him has to be mastered by the post man. He must know if the defensive center is playing him on the high side, low side, or sagging off way into the lane. Each of these is shown in Diagrams 11.4, 11.5, and 11.6.

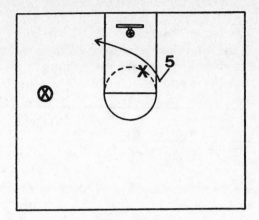

Diagram 11.4

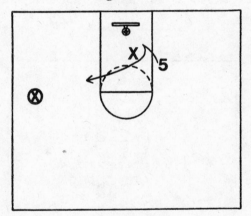

Diagram 11.5

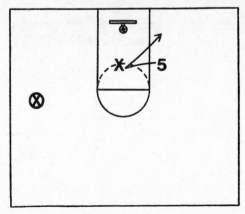

Diagram 11.6

If as in Diagram 11.4, the defensive post man is playing on the high side, then your post man must recognize this and move him higher to cut low toward the box along the lane. If, as in Diagram 11.5, the defender is on the low side, then the post man must take the defender low towards the baseline and make a good angle cut high toward the ball. If the defensive post man is sagging way off as in Diagram 11.6, then the post man must come directly to the ball, make contact with the defender, and expect a high lob pass over the top. Should the defense not react to any of the fakes, then the post man can use any moves to get open.

If two post men are employed in a high-low set, then each must play to and with each other. The phrase "buddy system" is appropriate here. The low post man screening for the high, the high post man screening for the low makes for a difficult assignment for the defense. Diagram 11.7 shows this.

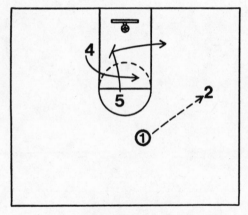

Diagram 11.7

Such a high-low system also enables the high post player to step out and reverse the ball. See Diagram 11.8. Many passing lanes are open from the point, especially if that point man happens to be a 6'2 or above player—one who can look over the defense better than a smaller man.

The post man doesn't have as many things to do in the passing game as the perimeter players. However, he must be smart, he must read defenses, and he must know when to roll ball-side, when to go weak-side, and when to screen and cut. He is still the hub of the attack because of his strategic position in the multi-purpose area.

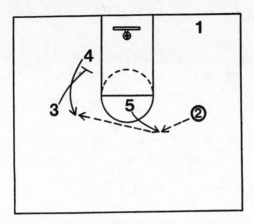

Diagram 11.8

POST RULES VERSUS THE ZONE DEFENSE

The general principles with which to attack the zone defense have been stated in previous chapters. Making the zone defense TILT to one side, FLOW in that direction, and then COUNTERING it to the opposite side is the most effective way to defeat zone defenses. Whenever the ball can be gotten into the multi-purpose area of the court, including especially the high post area, zone defenses become vulnerable.

General principles of the passing game or motion offense against the zone include the following:

1. Distort the zone with the initial alignment. If the zone is a two man front, go into a one man attack. If the zone is a one man front (1-3-1, 1-2-2), then go into a two guard attack.
2. Place a man always behind the back line of the zone. This man moves from side to side, pops out for the baseline jumper, or flashes to the middle.
3. Be prepared to dribble-penetrate the gaps and force a double-team or double-up on the ball. Be prepared to drop the pass off to an open man.
4. Reverse the ball from the top of the key against the zone. Thus, it is important in a motion offense to always have someone at or near the top of the circle.
5. Screen the zone, especially the weak side and throw the ball across court.
6. Constant ball-faking forces the zone to react and flow.

7. Never take a shot against the zone unless the post has handled the ball.

This last principle brings us to the post man's role in the passing game against a zone defense. By jamming the ball into the post man along or in the multi-purpose area, the defense is forced to collapse. This will free teammates for an open jumper. Therefore, it is of utmost importance for the post man to be able to catch the ball, pivot, and find the open seams of the zone. Obviously, when the post man receives the ball, he should look to shoot first. If the shot isn't there, he looks to pass. If the alignment is a two post offensive alignment, then he should look to his "buddy" first. If a single post set, then he looks to the open gaps.

Against the zone, the post man need not be as active as against the man to man. With a team that moves the ball well, the post man might just find himself running from side to side, trying to catch up with the ball. Therefore, the post man must anticipate his teammates' passes. As the ball is reversed (when he is on the weak-side), he should move the defense into the lane and then be prepared to catch the ball *along* the lane, as it is reversed to his side. See Diagram 11.9. #5, the post man, does not follow the ball from side to side but waits until it comes to him.

The post man must have a special knack of knowing where the open spots are and getting to them, should a perimeter player dribble-penetrate the zone defense and force a double team. The post man will become the recipient of many passes for easy layups if he masters this technique. Most of the time, the area opposite the dribble-penetrator will be open. So the post man must get to that area. Diagram 11.10 shows the post man filtering behind the defense towards the box opposite the dribble-penetration by player #3.

There are very few set rules to help the post man against zone defenses. Recognition and timing in practice situations, plus the knowledge of his teammates' abilities, best helps the post man to determine where to go in dribble-penetration situations.

Another secret tip that will help the post man in attacking zone defenses from a motion game offense is that he should always be looking weak side after catching the ball and failing to get a shot. Remember that the zone has tilted, flowed, and collapsed. Now it is vulnerable to a quick pass from the post to the weak side. Diagram 11.11 indicates this.

And finally, many hours have to be spent on offensive rebounding against the zone defense. Zones are susceptible to second and third shots because each player in the zone does *not* have a definite block-out re-

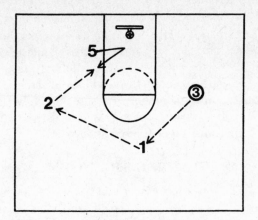

Diagram 11.9

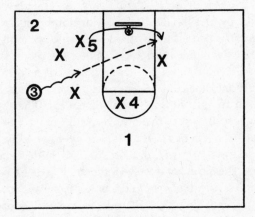

Diagram 11.10

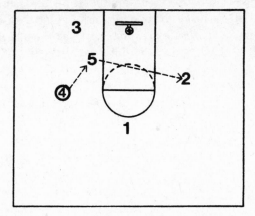

Diagram 11.11

sponsibility. Shooting the gaps between defenders who are screening out in an area rather than a particular man is a process that has to be practiced and practiced before it can be effectively mastered.

These are just a few ideas on using the post man in a motion offense against the zone. None of them will be effective unless the post man knows how to position himself and use his body, how to give a proper target, how to receive the pass, how to square up after reception, how to pass off, and how to get the offensive boards.

TIPS ON TEACHING THE PASSING GAME

A good practice philosophy is to make it more difficult in practice than it will be in the game. This forces concentration by the offense at all times.

Eventually work your way up to five offensive players against six defenders. Do this by first having 3 go against none. Let the three players practice passing game principles with no defensive men on them. Watch their cuts, their angles, their movement. When the coach is satisfied that they have down the principles, put three defensive men on them. Then go four against none, making one a post player. When satisfied with the movement and recognition, add four defenders. Then go five against none, eventually leading up to five on five. And finally, put six defenders on the court and have them go against five offensive players.

To force the post man to work on his moves, don't allow the ball to be shot unless the post has received the ball at least once. Or don't allow a shot, unless the pass or feed comes from the post man. It is good to scrimmage with this idea: the post man must shoot a layup only. This restriction really forces the post man to work to get open. Or no shot is to be taken until everyone on the team has handled the ball twice. Such restrictions make the offense work harder than they normally would in a game. There will be game slippage. So overcoaching and overemphasis in practice will do nothing but help the offense in game situations.

No matter what type of offense you decide to run—patterned or motion—the role of the post man does not differ that much. He is the focal point of the offense. He will make or break the team by the way he is used and by what he does.

12

DEVELOPING THE TOTAL POST GAME

Besides the individual mechanics of post play and the development of the post player into an offensive system, the complete post player still must be drilled in other facets of the game. The coach who wishes to implement a comprehensive system of basketball built around strong post play must give time and attention to other phases of player and team development.

Specific work on shooting and free throwing is a must. Determining to use the post man most effectively in a delay situation is necessary, or the post man may have to come out when you go into a stall or delay. How to use the post man against pressing defenses and how to align him in specialty situations, such as jump balls or last second shot situations, are all part of a coach's total master plan. If the coach has built a half court offense around the post player, then surely that coach will have to structure these other situations around the player too.

Individually speaking, the complete offensive post player has a vast collection of shots and moves. Although many teams will play (and be successful) with a post man who is a poor shooter but an effective rebounder and passer, shooting skills will make the post player a real threat and turn a good team into a great team, turn a good post man into a great one.

On a team basis, the complete post player not only can function against a man-to-man defense or against a zone defense, but is also the focal point of the delay game and the press attack against pressure defenses. Prudent use of the post man in the delay game and press attack is as important to winning as the fast break or regular team offense. In many ways, the coach who emphasizes the so-called "little things" or "specialty situations" of basketball comes out ahead in the long run.

SHOOTING DRILLS FOR THE POST MAN

What makes a good shooter? The traditional answer emphasized good form and technique with countless hours of long, hard practice. But how many players who practice long and hard and shoot the ball with

161

good form can't stick it in the net 8 p.m. on Friday night? All coaches have at some time or another experienced this. It is very frustrating for the individual who has the good form and has practiced long and hard to still be a poor shooter.

There has to be another element connected with shooting. Perhaps that missing element can best be labelled "THE MENTAL GAME." What the shooter thinks of himself, his self-image, is important. Total concentration on scoring, not being distracted by the defense, by fear of having a shot blocked, by the fear of missing, or by fatigue are all part of this MENTAL GAME.

Since the post man, of all the players on the court, will rarely if ever have a completely unmolested shot, this mental approach to shooting applies mainly to him.

What can coaches do about the mental game of the shooter? Talking about the mental approach to shooting, emphasizing concentration, positive thinking, encouraging, and complimenting are all part of helping the shooter's image of himself. Explaining to each player what is a good shot and a poor shot *for him* is another aspect of the mental game. Refraining from yanking a player for missing a shot does wonders for one's ego. In coaching situations, creating shooting drills that have distractions in them is essential.

The following drills are designed especially for the post man. They emphasize the shots and moves that the complete post player needs to operate effectively in the multi-purpose area. Some of them also incorporate the idea of working on the MENTAL APPROACH to shooting, assuming that the player has good form and wants to make an effort to become a good shooter.

Chapter 6 explained the "Super 11 Sequence" shooting drill. This series was designed to help offensive rebounding techniques and power moves inside. A review of these will reinforce their importance in developing an effective inside game for the post man.

Bank Jumper from Box. Diagram 12.1 shows the post man turning toward the baseline to bank in the baby jumper. The drill should be run at full speed, with the post man following each shot, not allowing the ball to hit the floor. He should alternate from the left to right side.

Swing Jumper into Middle. The post man steps into the lane, squares himself, and shoots the 8-10 foot jumper. He alternates sides, so that he is pivoting off both the right foot and the left foot. This move is employed when the defense is siding from the baseline side. Warding the defense with the off arm, the post man swings to the middle of the lane. The ideal practice set-up is shown in Diagram 12.2.

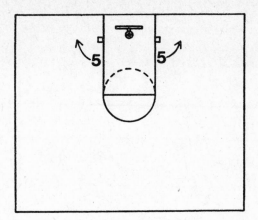

Diagram 12.1

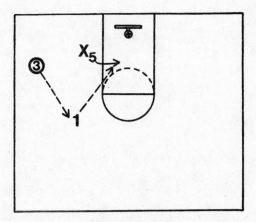

Diagram 12.2

Pounding Drill. This is a 1-on-1 drill with the offensive man starting with the ball at the box. No dribble is allowed. The defense can get physical—almost anything short of mayhem. The offensive man is encouraged to go towards the hoop, not away from it, and to use the pump fake as a means to draw the defense into an error.

Horizontal Slide into Middle. Moving up to the mid-post area, the player takes one hard, quick dribble into the middle for a short jumper, short hook, or lunging power layup. Diagram 12.3 shows this move.

Vertical Slide Down Lane. One quick dribble down the lane, with a good pump fake and taking the ball up tough as in the "pounding drill" are the ingredients for this drill. See Diagram 12.4.

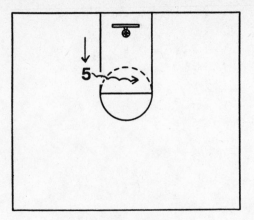

Diagram 12.3

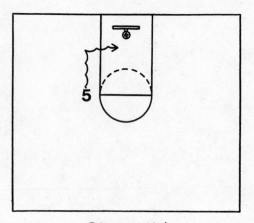

Diagram 12.4

Horizontal Slide with Reverse Dribble. Post man starts into lane with a dribble, picks the ball up, and reverses back toward the lane to shoot the jumper. Making the move with quickness and keeping the head up to prevent sagging defenders from swiping the ball are the keys to this move.

Vertical Slide with Reverse Dribble. Starting along the lane near the free throw line, the post man dribble-drives down the lane and makes a quick reverse dribble into the middle for the short hook or turn-around jumper. See Diagram 12.5.

High Post Moves. From the free throw line, the post man has to be able to shoot the turn-around jumper, to dribble-drive down the lane, and to drop step and drive to the basket.

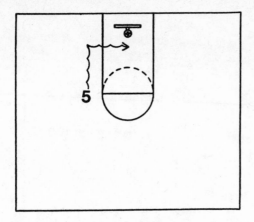

Diagram 12.5

Half Way Shooting Drills

Too often players practice from the 10-15 foot range. There is nothing wrong with this. But there are spots on the court from which players rarely practice. These are called the "half way" spots. Generally, they are 6-8 ft. from the basket. Some coaches call them the "baby" jump spot. For the post man these are along the baseline and inside the multi-purpose area in front of the hoop. When in the lane, 6 feet or so directly in front of the basket, make the post man bank the ball off the boards at all times. This is too close to the hoop to try to arch it directly over the front rim. Only by practicing from these "half way" spots will the player have confidence and know-how to bang these in during the game.

Pressure Against the Clock Shooting Drills

When most players practice shooting, they do so very slowly and lazily. They shoot the ball and walk in to get the ball back, slowly amble back to a spot and repeat the process. They really aren't getting much done. With this in mind, it is important to try to create some pressure on the shooter. This can be done effectively with the stop watch. Here are several drills employing this technique.

Machine Gun Drill. Two rebounders are lined up as shown in the Diagram 12.6. The post man starts at a designated spot. He is to only shoot from that spot on either side of the lane. He shoots for 30 seconds or whatever time the coach designates. The number of shots he takes and the number of shots he makes are charted. Each rebounder has a ball and alternates passing it to the post man, so he always has a ball to shoot.

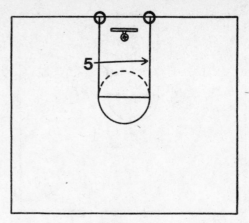

Diagram 12.6

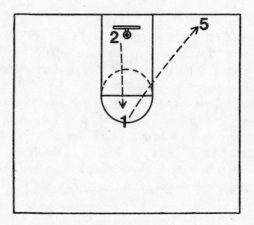

Diagram 12.7

3 man Shooting Drill. The setup of this drill is shown in Diagram 12.7. There are two balls at each basket. Player #1 will always pass to the shooter, player #5. Player #2 will rebound and pass to player #1. #1's job is to supply the shooter with a ball as soon as he hits the floor. All shots are charted. If a player can get off 30 shots in a minute, he and his partners have done a good job. Vary the drill by forcing the shooter to take one dribble. Getting off 20 shots from the dribble is excellent. Naturally, it is important to hit a good percentage of those shots taken. The advantage of this drill is that it is a "team" effort as all three men have to do their job and react to the shooter. The rebounder must not let the shot hit the floor, and the passer must make good passes to the shooter.

Distraction Shooting Drills

As implied earlier in this chapter, good shooting is simply "not being distracted by the defense, the crowd, the situation." Poor shooting is the opposite. Another way to put it is this: GOOD DEFENSE is "being able to distract the shooter." With this in mind, it is necessary to create distractions for the shooter. The hand in the face is one way to distract the shooter. All of the drills described in this chapter can be varied or adapted to a defender with his hand in the shooter's face. Another good distraction is to "bump" the shooter. Basketball is a contact game. Often times a shooter gets bumped, ever so slightly, as he gets into his shot. Using a football hand dummy to bump the shooter adds an element to any shooting drill that breaks some of the shooter's concentration. Just by having a defender standing next to a shooter with a hand dummy makes that shooter worry and does break some concentration.

If you have a big post man, use a broomstick to make him concentrate more on the basket. Sometimes a big post man has no one to contest him in practice as he gets into his shot. A 5'10 defender with a broomstick all of a sudden becomes 6'10.

A final distraction for the shooter is FATIGUE. It is wise to end practice with some type of shooting drill after doing some running or conditioning drill to bring about fatigue. Forcing the shooter to concentrate when tired is important to many game outcomes late in the fourth quarter.

There are hundreds of shooting drills for the post men. Two ideas are essential in developing drills that will benefit your post player. (1) Make sure that the drill works on the shot that the post man in your offense needs to develop. (2) Make sure that there is some type of pressure or distraction upon the post man as he works on the drill: time, hand in the face, being bumped, fatigue, or whatever.

DELAY GAME

The delay game is not a freeze or a stall. Rather it is a style of play which consumes time while drawing the opposition into defensive errors resulting in a score or a foul shot for the offense. Some coaches do not believe in a delay game. If their team has a 3-4 point lead with 40 seconds to play, they believe the 20 foot jump shot will go in. The choice and decision is yours.

Any type of delay game would probably be difficult to execute at the junior high level because youngsters at that age lack basic ball-handling (dribbling and passing) skills. This makes a delay game somewhat vulnerable to aggressive defense and pressure. The same problem is not as relevant at the high school and college levels.

There are two basic types of delay games: dribbling delays and passing delays, though some teams do combine each. The role of the post man in the dribbling delay is not as important as his role in a passing delay. The basic dribbling delay is the spread or 4-corner. In this delay, the post man lines up along the baseline and usually does not handle the ball unless he is on the scoring end of a pass from the quarterback or point man. Diagram 12.8 shows the initial alignment of the 4-corner delay.

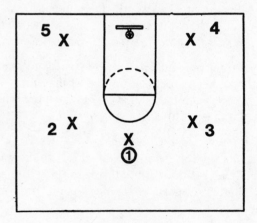

Diagram 12.8

The major role of the post man in this delay is to be able to cut to the basket when his defender leaves him to stop dribble penetration by one of the outside men. He must be able to shoot the power layup or at least draw the foul and get to the free throw line. Diagram 12.9 shows this basic concept of the 4-corner delay.

Spread or Passing Delay. The basic concept of this delay is to spread the defense so that a *cutter* can receive a pass from a teammate to go to the basket. The post man takes on a very significant role in this type of delay. He usually has to do much of the ball-handling, since positions are rotated because of the cutters. It is often advisable to have the post man (who is usually the biggest man on the team) handle the ball a lot because he will draw the opponent's biggest player to cover him. Thus the intimidator or shot blocker for the defense can be drawn away from the basket and pave the way for cutters. Diagram 12.10 shows the basic set-up of the spread/passing delay.

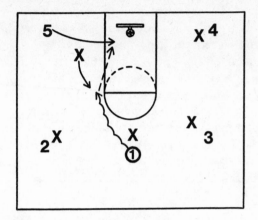

Diagram 12.9

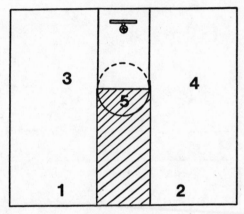

Diagram 12.10

The post man's area of concern is shown as the shaded area in the diagram. Players #1 and #2 are positioned about 1 step from the mid-court and 2-3 steps from the sideline. Players #3 and #4 (inside men) are positioned about a step or so below the free throw line. Be careful not to allow them to get too deep and pinned along the baseline. They should be this high on the court in order to vacate the basket area for cutters and for back door plays. #5, the middle man, is the post man. He should be at the free throw line in the initial lineup and be ready to operate down the lane in the multi-purpose area or as high as he needs toward the ten second line. His basic rule is to position himself always one pass away from the ball. The entire team must remember to stay spread out and utilize the entire floor. Players should not stand so close to a teammate that one defender could cover two men.

There are two basic passes and two basic cuts to be made in this delay. The first is a pass to an inside man and a cut by the outside man to the basket. This is shown in Diagram 12.11.

The post man and the two weak-side players must move their men. The weak-side men simply exchange (#2 and #4), while the post man must move his man in whatever direction will open the lane for the cutter. Should #5's defensive man sag off to stop the cutter (#1), then the post man pops out toward the 10 second line, while #3 dribbles out toward the 10 second line. #3 then hits #5 with a pass and this begins the second basic pass and cut in the delay. See Diagram 12.12.

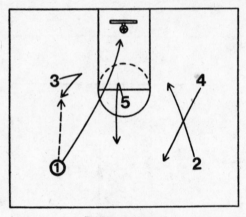

Diagram 12.11

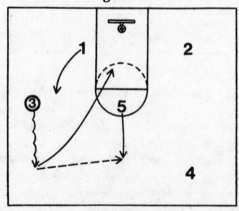

Diagram 12.12

The second basic option pass and cut off this spread delay is the pass to the middle man and the sucker cut or back door cut. Diagram 12.13 shows the sucker cut, while Diagram 12.14 the back door cut. Both cuts emphasize the importance of the post man and his ability to pass the ball.

When to use each cut is predicated upon hours of practice. Both the post man and the cutter have to read the defense and react accordingly. On the back door cut, the weak-side people have to clear the area.

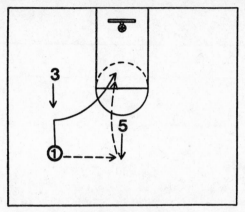

Diagram 12.13

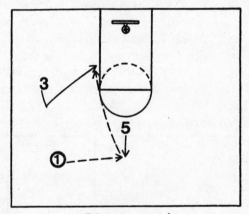

Diagram 12.14

All three of these moves are incorporated into the spread delay pattern. If the post man will work both sides of the court, it is very difficult for the defense to stop the layup. The post man must be constantly in motion. He will not be moving a great distance, but will be head and shoulder faking, quickly, in and out, towards the basket and away from the basket. His ability to get open is the key to reversing the ball and working both sides of the court. Should the defensive post man really overplay and not go for any fake towards the basket, then the post man has to be ready to burn him. This can be keyed by a voice command, a raised arm, or simply by eye contact with the passer. The movement is shown in Diagram 12.15.

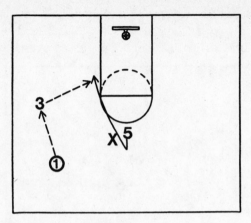

Diagram 12.15

In the diagram, #5 is being overplayed by X, his defender. Outside player #1 passes up court to #3 but, because the play has been keyed, #1 does not cut. Instead, the post man gives a fake towards the 10-second line as if he were coming out to get open to receive the pass but suddenly cuts down the lane ball-side for a quick pass from #3.

Another way to run the same play is to pass the ball directly from the outside man over-the-top to the post man cutting down the lane. Obviously this pass is more dangerous than the shorter pass from the inside man. Diagram 12.16 shows this.

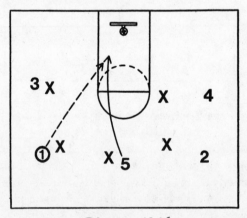

Diagram 12.16

A basic rule that applies to anyone who has the ball is this: if in trouble, dribble at someone, forcing a clear out. Thus, if the post man has the ball in the middle near the 10-second line and everyone is covered, he should take one or two dribbles at an outside player, forcing that player to cut toward the hoop and bringing the inside man out toward the 10-second line. This is diagrammed in 12.17. A ball fake at the outside will serve the same purpose: force that man being faked at to cut to the hoop. This action moves the defense and usually results in the freeing of one or another teammate for a release pass.

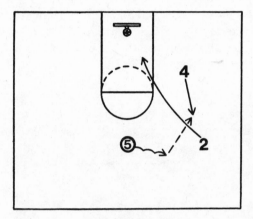

Diagram 12.17

It is important to note that if the defense is sagging and jamming the middle to cover the cutters, there is no way that they will ever get the ball. The offense should be content to pass the ball around the perimeter. Remember: the offense has the lead and will maintain that lead in this delay game. If the defense is out covering the offense, pressuring the ball, then the delay game HAS to look for the layup. THIS OFFENSE IS NOT A STALL. This type of offense runs into trouble when players forget that they are looking for a layup. Conservative play when pressured results in turnovers and loss of the lead. Play aggressively in the spread delay and the offense will keep the pressure on the defense.

The role of the post man in this system is crucial. His presence on the court forces the defense to keep their post man out there. If a team substitutes a small guard to harass the post man, then the offense will have to run the bigger post man down to the box and jam the ball into him. If the defense keeps its regular post man out on defense, then the middle is open for cutters. The post man's ability to pass, to move his man, to dribble, and to read defenses is of utmost importance to the success of this system. But, as has been emphasized throughout this entire book, these skills or abilities are central to the success of any offense which employs a post player.

PRESS ATTACK

In keeping with the basic idea of simplicity, a coach should devise one press attack to attack all pressing defenses. There seems to be little doubt that the press thrives on teams that try to dribble the ball up against it. Teams that attack the press with short, crisp passes are most successful.

The fast break attack goes hand-in-hand with the press offense. Recall in Chapter 7 the method for the transitional break. A release guard flies downcourt on the shot, while the second guard goes to the outlet area. One of the frontliners takes the ball out of bounds, while the other two frontliners take the third lane or the trailer position. When the offense sees that the defense has set up a full court press, slight adjustments will be made.

Diagram 12.18 shows the basic concept of the transitional break. After the ball has gone through the net, player #3 takes the ball out of bounds.

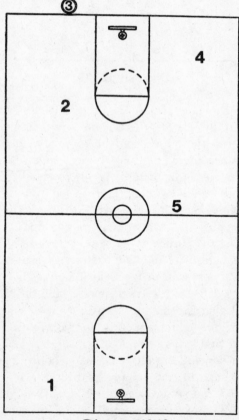

Diagram 12.18

The press offense is an attack built upon the idea of filling five designated spots on the playing court. Those are: BALL, LAG MAN, MIDDLE MAN, UP COURT, DEEP OPPOSITE. Any player can fill any one of these spots. However, because of the nature of the transitional break, certain players will generally line up in specific spots, with the post man usually taking the MIDDLE MAN spot.

A definition of these positions is in order:

BALL—refers to the man with the basketball.

LAG MAN—refers to a player who is one step behind the line of the ball. He is an outlet man should the ball man be stopped; he acts as a safety valve.

MIDDLE MAN—refers to a player, usually the post man, who occupies the middle of the court.

UP COURT—refers to a player along the sideline who is on the ball side of the court. He is usually 20-30 feet away from the man with the ball.

DEEP OPPOSITE—refers to a player who is at the extreme end of the court away from the side of the ball.

In Diagram 12.19, #2 is the BALL MAN, #3 is the LAG MAN, #5 is the MIDDLE MAN, #1 is the UP COURT, and #4 is the DEEP OPPOSITE PLAYER. Compare Diagram 12.19 with Diagram 12.18 to see how the players on the transitional break react when they determine that a press defense has been set up against them.

The basic idea of the press offense is to keep these five spots filled until a breakdown of the defense occurs. Such a breakdown will occur when the ball is either into the middle (where #5, the post man is) or when the ball is passed across the 10-second line and the offense outnumbers the defense.

The general philosophy of attacking a zone by making it TILT to one side, FLOW, and then COUNTERING it to the other is still employed in this situation, since most presses have elements of zoning to them.

If the offense can beat the press before it gets set up (and there is a good chance of doing this by releasing a guard long and working hard on the transitional game and getting the ball in bounds quickly), then the pressing defense is relatively ineffective. If the press has gotten set up, a sure way to disrupt it is to get the ball into the middle man. For this reason, the post man represents an ideal middle man. He is well-schooled in the art of posting up, of keeping the defense behind him with body position. The post man is usually the tallest player on the court and hence makes a good target. The post man also has been taught to pivot when he receives the ball and look weak side after having received a pass. All of these traits should stand him in good stead against a press defense.

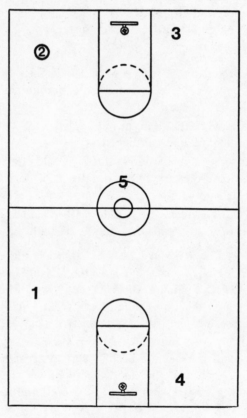

Diagram 12.19

The ideal situation is shown in Diagram 12.20. The ball is passed into the middle man who looks to the weak side to his teammates filling the open slots. The zone has flowed to one side but is now countered to the other. A quick one or two dribbles should result in a bucket. In keeping with the philosophy of aggressiveness, the offense should keep attacking the press. It should not just be content to get the ball across the 10-second line and then set up in its half court offense. This philosophy helps the pressing team take more chances on going for the ball. Keep going at the press, attacking it at all times. Be ready and prepared to take the shot on the 2-on-1, 3-on-2, and even a 3-on-3 situation.

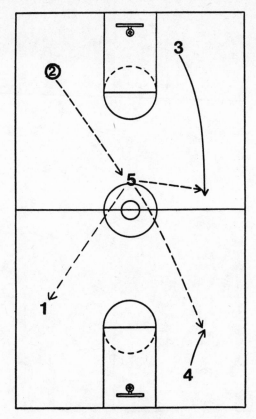

Diagram 12.20

Should the ball be passed from the BALL MAN to the UP COURT MAN, the post man flies down the middle looking for a return pass. See Diagram 12.21.

But perhaps the most effective method of attacking the press is the FLIP-FLOP method. This method really forces the zone defense to TILT and FLOW to one side, making it very susceptible to being COUNTERED on the other side. The action is shown in Diagram 12.22. As the BALL MAN throws the ball to the LAG MAN, the UP COURT (#1) and the DEEP OPPOSITE PLAYER (#4) flip flop positions. The UP COURT MAN goes to the DEEP OPPOSITE POSITION, while the DEEP OPPOSITE becomes the UP COURT. LAG MAN becomes the BALL MAN, while the BALL MAN now is the LAG MAN. The only constant is the middle man, #5, the post man.

With the pass from #2 to #3, the middle man may be open or #4, the new up court man rushing towards the 10-second line, may also be

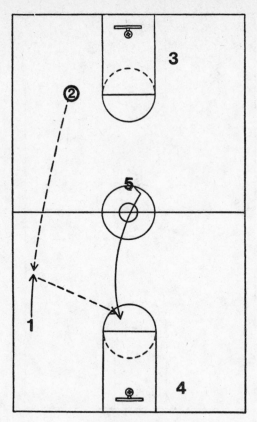

Diagram 12.21

open. And don't be too surprised if #1, moving behind the zone to the new **DEEP OPPOSITE** position, frees himself as the zone **FLOWS** to the ball side. If none of these options result in a pass being made forward, then the final option is invoked. Player #2 filters behind the **FLOWING** defense and frees himself for a countering cross-court pass. See Diagram 12.23. The pass from #3 to #2 is most unsuspected and is generally effective against any type of zone press. This is a great countering move against the flow of the defense. The defense is flowing to the right, reacting on the middle man and #4 as he comes bursting up toward the 10-second line. They tend to lose #2, who hesitates and slips in behind the defense.

In all of these maneuvers, the post man is crucial. His presence is imposing because he forces the zone to collapse in and around him. He is not to leave this area, even if double or triple-teamed. This doubling or tripling on the post man serves to free teammates in other

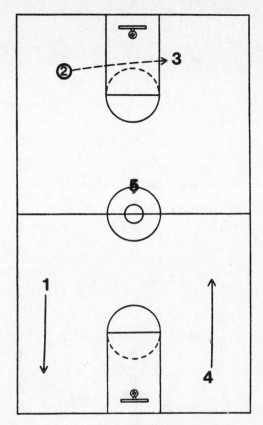

Diagram 12.22

positions. The post man must always position himself as if he were going to get the next pass. His arms should be outstretched towards the ball, whether it is coming to him or not. In other words, many times he is simply the decoy—but an effective decoy at that. And if he should receive the pass, his immediate task is to pivot hard and tough towards the middle, facing the goal and looking weak side for a teammate. The post man must not take more than 1 dribble out of this area because good pressing teams are taught to flow back on defense protecting the middle. Without hard work and effort from the middle man or post man, this press offense cannot succeed. With hard work and effort, this offense won't fail.

This offense is effective because it is simple and easy to learn. It is adaptable to any type of press defense, and it is also effective on a half court or three-quarters court basis. Simply apply the same principles and attack these presses the same way.

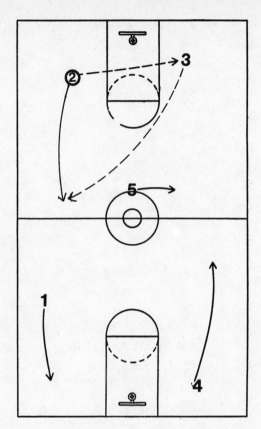

Diagram 12.23

FREE THROW ALIGNMENTS

Many coaches leave to chance the rebounding of missed free throws. Since the average number of free throws shot per game is between 15 and 20, missed free throws offer many opportunities for possession of the basketball. Each player on the court must know what is expected of him on the free throw alignment. Each player on the court must realize what game situation exists and what alignment must be employed to take advantage of that situation.

There are three basic free throw alignments: normal, gap, and safety. Each one of these is employed for a different purpose; each one is used in a specific situation. Since the post man is usually the best rebounder, he becomes a vital factor in each of these.

The "NORMAL" free throw alignments are shown below in Diagrams 12.24 and 12.25. Diagram 12.24 shows the normal defensive free throw alignment when the opposition is shooting the ball. Diagram

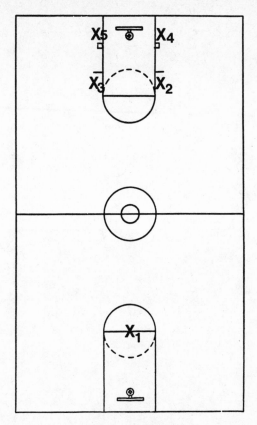

Diagram 12.24

12.25 shows the normal offensive free throw alignment when your team is shooting the ball.

The normal defensive alignment is used most frequently during the game. In Diagram 12.24, four rebounders are positioned along the free throw lane, with the best rebounders in positions inside the block, closest to the basket. The feet of X5 and X4 should be positioned as close to the block as possible. When the ball hits the rim, the leg and elbow farthest away from the rim should be extended sharply into the lane. Theoretically, the farthest leg of each inside rebounder should meet in the lane. Both are instructed to step at the shooter so as to wedge the men in the second slots out. Diagram 12.26 shows this step. Both should keep a wide base and their arms extended up in the air so that they can corral the flat shot that hits hard off the rim or the ball that caroms off to the side.

X3, as shown in Diagram 12.24, takes a position near the hash mark and forms the point of the rebounding triangle. His prime job is not

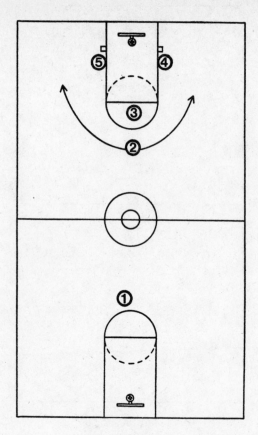

Diagram 12.25

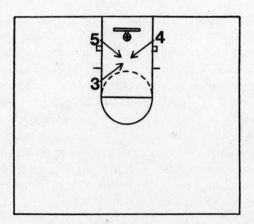

Diagram 12.26

to secure the ball, but keep the opponent in the second free throw slot from securing possession. In other words, he wedges that opponent out by stepping into the lane with his inside foot—the foot closest to the baseline. A quick referral to Diagram 12.26 will show X3's movement.

X2 lines up closest to the shooter, stationing himself on the shooter's shooting hand—in the case of Diagram 12.24, the shooter's right side. X2's job is a simple one, to block off the shooter from getting a rebound that caroms back toward him. Most good free throw shooters will not miss, if they miss at all, by much. They will usually miss short or slightly long in the middle so that the ball caroms back toward the lane. Good shooters won't be off to one side or the other, thus necessitating a rebound that caroms right off to the right side or to the left side. X1 is stationed back so that the shooting team is forced to commit at least one player back to match up with him, thereby reducing the shooting team to only three men along the lane. Also, a player back that far will put added pressure on the defense and help the rebounding team to run on the made or missed free throw.

The normal offensive rebound set as shown in Diagram 12.25 is based on the premise that you rarely get an offensive rebound on a free throw against a good team. The good team is so well-schooled in the art of blocking out, that only through a glaring mistake or lucky bounce will the offensive team get another shot at it.

With this in mind, the shooting team will place its two best rebounders in the second free throw slot, but be careful as to always place the best rebounder against the weaker of the opponents lined up in the first slot. Play the percentages. If your best rebounder is a 6'8 player, why line him up on the offensive free throw next to the 6'8 player from the other team? He'll most likely get the ball anyway if it's missed because he's in the first slot. Instead, line up your 6'8 rebounder against the smaller of the opposition. He'll have a better chance to get a missed shot. The weaker rebounder goes in the second slot next to the defensive team's strongest. Tell the offensive rebounder in this slot not to worry about getting the ball but instead try to harass the inside rebounder by hedging him, pushing a little, or interlocking his arms so that he can't sky to secure the ball. Both offensive rebounders in the second slot should line up right along the block, as close as they can get. They should thrust the leg and arm nearest the baseline into the lane first in order to try to beat the inside rebounder to the spot first.

The remaining players should line up as shown in Diagram 12.25, with O2 being given some free-lance opportunities to roam to where

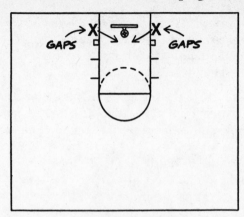

Diagram 12.27

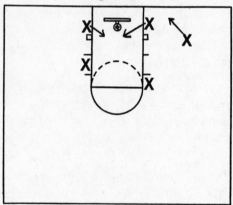

Diagram 12.28

he thinks the ball might carom. O1 is back as a safety against the break and his job is to build the defense.

The "GAP" alignment is used to take advantage of a team that blocks out so well that they give the inside gaps as shown in Diagram 12.27. It is also used against a shooter who is not a good free thrower and generally misses off to the side. The defensive gap set up is shown in Diagram 12.28, while the offensive gap set up is shown in Diagram 12.29. The GAP alignment is also effective against individuals who rebound and bring the ball down to their waist in a slow-type motion. It is easy to shoot the gap and tie such a player up for the jump ball.

The SAFETY free throw alignment is designed to create maximum opportunities to secure the ball, if on defense, and maximum protection against any type of break while on offense. Diagram 12.30 shows the defensive SAFETY alignment, while Diagram 12.31 shows the offensive SAFETY alignment.

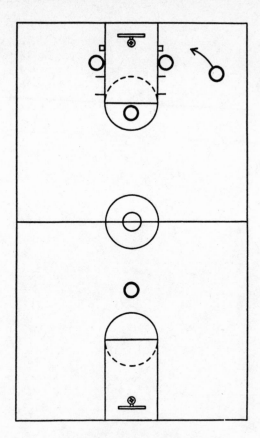

Diagram 12.29

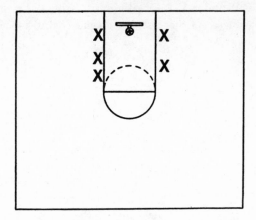

Diagram 12.30

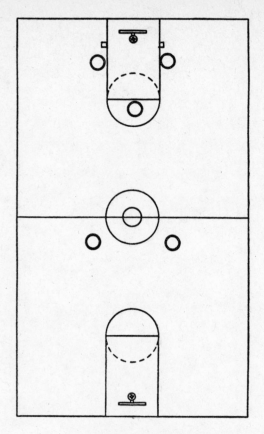

Diagram 12.31

Both the GAP and SAFETY alignments use the same basic techniques in rebounding from the first and second free throw slots along the
lane as in the NORMAL alignment.

LAST-SECOND SHOT PHILOSOPHY

Every team that is well-prepared will have a philosophy and series
of plays designed for last-second, last-shot usage. Depending on the
amount of time left at the end of the game, it is wise or unwise to try
to use the post man. With 10 seconds or less left on the clock, no matter
what the ability of the post man, try to get the shot up and allow the
post man to go to the weak side so that he can rebound. With more
than 10 seconds remaining, depending on the ability of the post man,
enough time is there to either go to the post man or not go to him.

POST MAN AND JUMP BALLS

Normally the post man will be the player who jumps center at the jump ball to begin each quarter. In coaching the jumper on the jump balls, it is important to make him aware of a number of simple concepts. First, look before entering the jump circle and have an idea of where to go with the ball. Second, never spike or hit the ball with the fist. Third, concentrate on the referee's motions and actions. He might tip off his hand as to when he'll release the ball. Fourth, concentrate on the height to which the official tosses the ball.

The objectives of any jump ball should, in order of importance, be:

1. Try to gain possession.
2. Prevent an easy score by the opposition.
3. Try to get a score.

On jump balls not involving the post man directly, the post man should always line up offensively. His presence in this position always poses a threat that must be countered with usually two defenders, especially if the post man is a great player, or tall and/or strong.

Since there are at least four jump balls in a given game (and usually eight to ten totally), it is wise to set up some type of strategy on the jump balls. Since the coach definitely knows who'll be his jumper at the start of each quarter and most likely knows who'll oppose that jumper, the coach should decide if he can get the tip, if it is definitely a loss tip, or if it is a toss-up—meaning his player might or might not secure the tip. Depending on this decision, a scoring play can be set up, rotation or movement of players off and around the circle can be planned, or a straight defensive tip can be planned.

In general, the more men on the jump ball circle, the less certainty there is that the tip will go where it is planned. If a team feels certain that it can get the tip, then it is wise to place only two men on the circle and station the other two players off the circle, perhaps even under the basket. Such a move forces the hand of the opposition. On the other hand, if a team feels that it most likely will not get the tip, then it would like to keep as many men on the circle as possible. The theory is that the more hands going for the ball, the more chances there are that it won't go where it is intended to go. Naturally, a game of cat-and-mouse can be played with this philosophy if both coaches are skilled and abide by the principles suggested herein.

FREE THROW SHOOTING

A sure fire way to determine whether or not the post man is an effective player is to determine how many free throw opportunities he has during a given year. As the hub of a team's offense and the focal point of the defense, the post man should go to the free throw line as much as any member of the squad. Therefore, it is very important for the post man to spend much time at the free throw line during practice.

Many teams and players waste time at the free throw line during practice sessions. Allowing players to stand at the line and shoot ten or twenty in a row, while talking and clowning with teammates, in no way simulates game conditions.

A few simple policies in regards to free throw shooting can help to create a more serious effort in practice. First, allow no one to talk at the free throw line. Second, a player only shoots until he makes two in a row. If he does this on his first two attempts, then another player steps to the line. Third, after shooting a free throw, the player must always step off the line. This is standard procedure under game conditions. It is ridiculous for a player to stand at the line and shoot ten or twenty consecutive free throws without moving, as his teammate feeds him. Fourth, poor free throw shooters never shoot with poor shooters. Psychologically, it is important for poorer shooters to shoot with good shooters. Just the idea of competing with a good shooter can spur on a poorer shooter to concentrate just a little bit more. Fifth, all free throw attempts are charted in practice by a student manager. Sixth, a player is instructed never to show any emotion at the line, whether he hits two in a row five consecutive times, or whether he misses both ends of the free throw attempt.

With these rules of procedure established, it is now important to shoot free throws with the proper technique. First and foremost is a set routine. All players should develop a routine—a set pattern or style—that they follow each time they go to the line. For some, it will mean stepping to the line, bouncing the ball three times, taking a deep breath to relax, pausing for two counts, and then shooting. Others will have a different routine. But since free throw shooting is pure habit, it is imperative to establish a habit and STICK WITH IT if the player is to develop into a great free throw shooter.

Once the routine has been established, then the player must have the proper form. Checkpoints include foot alignment, grip, elbow, and follow-through.

The final, and maybe the most important part of free throw shooting, is the mental approach to free throwing. The shooter's image of himself and the confidence that he has in his efforts are most important in the success of the free throw. The shooter can't be worried about a miss. He can't be worried about the pressure situation or the crowd.

He can't fear being chastised by the coach or his friends. He must feel that he is the best shooter in the gym, and he must want to go to the line. To achieve all of this, the shooter's concentration level must be so high that everything else has been blotted from his mind. In order to help the shooter's concentration, have him shoot five free throws with the coach standing over him urging him to watch the "orange" rim and ball as it comes through the net. After shooting these five free throws, have the shooter put the ball down on the floor and form shoot five. Have him go through his set routine as he shoots each one of these five. Obviously, he should make all five. Remind him to concentrate on the rim and to see the ball going through the net. After shooting these five without the ball, then have the player close his eyes and form shoot five more. The coach urges him at all times to see the orange rim and see the net swish up as the ball goes through. The player again takes his time and delivers the ball from his set routine and form. It might be added here that it is best to do this drill before or after practice when no one is around except the shooter and the coach. Concentration level is highest at this time as there are no distractions at all. After form shooting five with the eyes closed, the player now takes the ball and, with his eyes closed again, shoots five at the basket. The coach is there to encourage and assist him. Praise each shot whether it goes in, is close, or not. You might be surprised at the results of this. The player, if he is concentrating and if he has developed a rhythm and idea of where the rim is, will surprise himself with his accuracy. Finally, have the player open his eyes and shoot five regular free throws. In the final analysis, the player now will have shot 25 free throws. True, only ten of them will have been under normal game conditions—eyes open, with the ball, and the like. But the others will all have an element of concentration in them that is so important for successful free throwing.

A final free throw shooting drill that is designed for concentration purposes is simply called "CONCENTRATION." This drill is used as an incentive. Only if the player can consistently make 90% of his free throws in practice is he allowed to engage in this contest.

The basic premise behind "CONCENTRATION" is to hit the perfect shot. Coaches will disagree on what the perfect shot is. But let's assume that the perfect shot is one which hits the back part of the rim with a "THUD" sound, comes cleanly through the net as the net flies upward, and bounces back to the shooter at the free throw line. Diagram 12.32 shows the part of the rim where the ball strikes to become the "perfect" shot.

At this point, it is important to note that, as coaches, we'll take the ball going in *any way*—off the boards, bouncing off the rim, and so on. But for the purpose of this drill, try to achieve the perfect shot. Remember, this drill is not designed for the players who have trouble shooting free throws. Rather it is designed to improve the good free thrower and make him a great shooter—one who can hit 85-90% in game conditions. It is also fun for the athletes to participate in this drill.

For hitting the "perfect shot," a player gets 5 points. If the shooter "swishes" his shot, hitting nothing but net, he gets 4 points. If the made shot hits any part of the rim—front or side—the shooter gets 3 points. If the ball hits the rim, the backboard, and flops in, the shooter gets 2 points. If the shot goes in off the boards, then the shooter gets 1 point. If the shot is missed, no points are received. So in summary,

5 points for the perfect shot
4 points for a "swish" — all net
3 points for a made shot hitting any part of the iron
2 points for a shot that hits the rim, backboard, and in
1 point for a shot off the boards
0 points for a miss

The shooter fires five shots, keeping score of his points. Any score over 20 is super. Most players will hit around 13-17 points. The game is fun and is a *privilege* for those free throwers who can constantly hit 85-90% in practice. Don't allow poorer shooters the privilege of this competition during practice. Remember, the ultimate purpose of the drill is to get the shooter to concentrate totally on that back part of the orange rim so that he can hit the "perfect" shot.

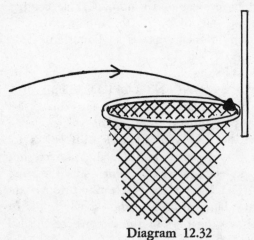

Diagram 12.32

13

DEFENSIVE POST PLAY

As the years pass and one gains experience as a coach, he begins to realize that the game of basketball is much simpler than one had previously tried to make it. Many young coaches out of college come into the game with great ideas and expectations. They think that they know it all and wish to impart all of this vast amount of knowledge to their players. Little do they realize that, although coaches think a lot about the game of basketball, most players do not. They think about basketball only for the two hours or so that they practice or play in game competition.

Because of the small amount of time available to teach and coach compared to the vast amount of knowledge and skills needed to be taught to the individual players, it is very important to simplify the game as much as possible. If a player understands the theory and philosophy behind a given drill or a specific play, it will be easier for him to accomplish it on the court. So, with that in mind, defense—a very difficult but extremely necessary part of the game—has to be made as simple as possible.

Instead of talking about which foot to put forward when sliding, whether or not to swipe with the arm or keep it back, or similar defensive coaching tips, it is much more basic to give the players some simple rules of general defense and then break down the rules to get to the fundamentals of defense. By doing this, your defense will be fairly effective and this, in turn, will allow more time to concentrate on offensive fundamentals which are more difficult to master because the basketball is involved directly with the players.

GENERAL RULES FOR DEFENSE

The rules that follow are general team defensive rules. But obviously, since the post man plays in the multi-purpose area and is the hub of the defense by his central location on the court, he has to be especially concerned with mastery of the philosophy and then the techniques.

Defensive Rule #1. Guard the Basket

The object of the game is to put the ball in the hoop. All players should be instructed to stop the opponents from scoring. If a player has the choice of guarding his man, his area, or the basket, he is always instructed to guard the basket. Because of this rule, you should not give up too many layups during a game. Whenever you can force the opposition to beat you with the jumper rather than the layup, you have greatly enhanced your opportunity to win.

Defensive Rule #2. Guard the Ball

Once the basket is guarded and covered, one must find the ball and guard it. A rather simple concept, but, I ask you, how do you explain it to your players? Following naturally from these first two principles, then, would be the idea that you stay between your man and the basket while on defense.

Defensive Rule #3. Don't Let the Opposition Throw the Ball Where They Want To

Usually after several minutes of the game it is rather obvious how a team is going to attack. The coach must then communicate to his players that the ball must be thrown to areas other than those where the defense wants to throw it.

Defensive Rule #4. Always Keep a Hand Up on the Shooter

It is not a natural act to hold one's arms up in the air. But GOOD SHOOTING is simply "not being distracted by the defense." GOOD DEFENSE is being "able to distract the shooter." The arm in the air is the best means of distraction to the shooter. Coaches should do a lot of work in this area. As mentioned earlier, run drills that require the arms to be kept up. Run sprints with the arms up. Never shoot in pre-practice sessions without a defender's hand in the shooter's face. When one player hits the floor for practice, he may shoot; but when another player comes onto the floor, then the two must pair off and go to work on defensing each other's shots.

Defensive Rule #5. Don't Foul

This goes hand in hand with rule #4. Constantly preach to your players that the opponents must beat you from the floor. Constantly yell in practice "DON'T FOUL." This is so important when playing the shooter. Rarely talk about trying to block shots. There just aren't many clean blocks allowed by the referees in basketball today. The defensive man on the shooter must be told to concentrate on two things:

1. Be the second man off the floor on a jumper.
2. Keep his arm straight up—not out and then letting it fall forward.

Most shooting drills should be designed with a defender against the shooter so that a good habit of contesting the shooter can be built up. If you do not send the opponents to the free throw line and keep them from the layup (as mentioned in Rule #1), you will win a great majority of your games.

Defensive Rule #6. Don't Give Up the Second Shot

Obviously, here we are talking about a most important phase of defense—rebounding. Simply put: if you give the opponents second and third attempts, most will not score on the initial shot. Hence, victory will be within your grasp. Chapter 6 on rebounding spells out some specifics used to teach good rebounding techniques.

Defensive Rule #7. Make Your Opponent Beat You with the Jumper

This has been mentioned several times before, but it is so important that it bears repetition. Shot charts and statistics can help you determine how successful your defense has been in maintaining these rules.

So in summary, defense can be taught simply from a basic philosophy which emphasizes seven rules:

1. Guard the basket.
2. Guard the ball.
3. Don't let the opponents throw the ball where they want to.
4. Keep a hand up on the shooter.
5. Don't foul.
6. Don't give up the second shot.
7. Make the opposition beat you with the jumper.

Without a philosophy or idea of what defense is supposed to accomplish, all the preceding information is no good. With these seven rules, players can readily understand what defense is all about. There is little doubt that if a player gets loose and heads to the basket with the ball, every other defensive man must be ready to help stop the offensive drive because RULE #1 is to "GUARD THE BASKET."

All players should be able to understand and recite these rather simple concepts which are so important in playing good defense.

Especially should the post man be knowledgeable about these principles. He is the man in the middle. He is the man most often called upon to guard the basket and leave his man to do so. He is the man who most often has to contest a shooter. He is the man who frequently has the opportunity to get himself in foul trouble. He is the man at the hub of your defense who must solidify the entire team defense.

RULES FOR ONE-ON-ONE
HALF COURT DEFENSE

Having experienced the general principles of overall defense, it is now mandatory to try to make individual one-on-one defense as simple as possible. This too must be communicated in simplified terms, in the hope that the youngsters come away with the idea that it can be accomplished because they fully understand what is expected of them.

The rules for one-on-one half court defense are these:

Rule #1. Pressure the Ball.

Rule #2. Prevent Change of Direction of the Ball, Unless Done Over the Defender's Head. In other words, don't allow the offensive man with the ball to fake from side to side. This can be prevented by positioning the arm directly in front at the midsection of the offensive player. Force that offensive player to keep the ball on one side of his body.

Rule #3. Don't Allow an On-Side Move—Make the Offensive Player Use the Crossover. This is important for two reasons: first, crossovers are much more difficult to master; second, crossovers are often called "steps" or "travelling" by the officials.

Rule #4. Don't Go for Any Lateral Fakes; Only React to Fakes Toward the Basket.

Rule #5. Defensive Players Must Fake Just Like Offensive Players Do. Teach defenders to stunt, shout, harass the opposition so that the offensive player is off guard and worried about his defender.

Rule #6. Defensive Man Should Always Be the Second Man Off the Floor on a Shot.

Now realize that what has been said is not revolutionary or new but is SIMPLE. The game has to be kept this way so that those playing it can enjoy it to its fullest. The root of any successful coach, team, or program is a sound, simple philosophy with simple teaching mechanisms to get defensive points across.

REMEMBER: Simple concepts on defense, taught simply and understood by all, can produce winners.

POST MAN AND HALF COURT TEAM
DEFENSIVE STRATEGY

As part of the total team defensive picture, a basic philosophy of defensive strategy must be developed on a half court basis. The post man becomes the key determinant of such a philosophy. If the post man is a well-rounded player—strong physically, quick reacting, good jumper, intelligent, and a good defensive player—then it becomes sound practice to push or influence the basketball to the middle of the court. Pushing the ball to the middle of the court demands that each defender know how to overplay one step to the outside, thus influencing the ball towards the multi-purpose area. Especially if the post man is a big, strong specimen (6'7 or bigger) is this strategy effective. The post man thus becomes an intimidator.

Many coaches disagree about pushing the ball into the middle of the court, saying that the ball is being driven toward the basket. However, an intimidating post man stationed in the multi-purpose area forces the offense to commit many dribbling, passing and shooting errors, thus creating many more possessions for his team. Recalling the basic principles of defense, the post man should never give up a layup and always encourage the offense to take a jumper under pressure from the outstretched arm. Since every member of the team has been schooled in this philosophy and realize what the half court defense is trying to achieve, the "push to the middle" strategy becomes much more effective.

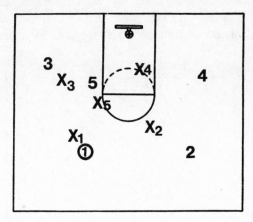

Diagram 13.1

If the defense is set up man-to-man, the alignment will be somewhat as described in Diagram 13.1. Against a traditional 2-1-2 offensive attack, defender X1 overplays the outside and gets support from his

strong side (ball-side) forward X3, who clogs the passing lane from #1
to #3. X4 is in a help position clogging the multi-purpose area, while
X2 stations himself in such a way that he can double team #1 should
he dribble-drive to the middle. Thus offensive guard #2 becomes the
next logical receiver. Diagram 13.2 shows the movement of personnel
when the pass is made to guard #2.

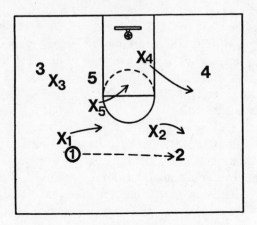

Diagram 13.2

The overplay of the strong-side forward should force the guard out
front with the ball to try to make the back door pass to his strong-side
forward, which is one of the most difficult passes in the game to
execute or dribble-drive the middle, where the defensive post man will
be waiting to intimidate. Diagram 13.3 shows this move.

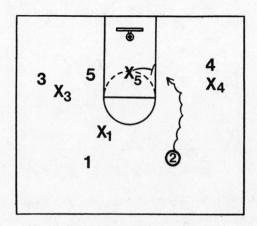

Diagram 13.3

Even if the ball does get to the forward spot, the philosophy of driving the ball to the middle remains the same. Diagram 13.4 shows this. X4 plays the ball in such a manner that the only avenue of dribble-drive open to offensive player #4 is toward the middle where X1 and the post man, X5, are ready to converge and help. More likely than not the ball will have to be passed back out to the guard spot. It is true that perhaps the guard will have the 18 foot jumper. But this shot will not consistently beat you, whereas the layup or inside power shots will.

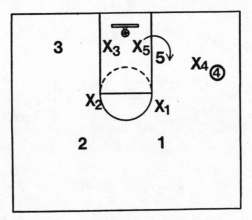

Diagram 13.4

To make such a defense effective, whether it be in a man or zone, hours of practice must be devoted to the team game. Daily work, however, must be done with the post man since he is the hub of the defense —in many cases, the last line of defense. The post man must be able to play 2 against 1, even at times, 3 against 1. It is important to make the post man play against such odds in practice. The half court 3 on 1, or 2 on 1 drills with the post man being the pivot man back in the middle are especially effective. Diagram 13.5 shows this.

The post man should recall his first rule of defense: guard the basket. Thus, he should not allow the layup and in such situations should always try to get a hand up on the shooter, without giving up the inside shot.

Needless to say, the post man must be agile and quick reacting with his hands. Passing drills, such as *"bull in the ring"* (see Diagram 13.6) are effective to develop these skills. All the post man has to do in this drill is to *touch the pass.*

A similar drill is the "TOUCH PASSING DRILL." This drill combines the ideas of guarding the basket, yet challenging the ball-handler to deflect a pass. It forces the post man to make a quick judgement and then react. The alignment is shown in Diagram 13.7. The line of guards out front with the basketball dribble into the top of the circle area. As soon as the guard hits this area, the post man can challenge the ball. The guard with the ball must stop between the top of the key and the free throw line. He MUST STOP. This area is shaded on the Diagram 13.7. Knowing this, the post man can challenge him in this area. All he must do is to touch the ball to be successful. Once the post man touches the ball, the drill ends.

The post man may stunt at the dribbler and fade back to play the other offensive player who is stationed at the box. That offensive player cannot move from that spot. If this happens, the dribbler can either shoot or attempt a quick pass to the player on the box. Either way the post man reacts. The drill encourages quick thinking, quick feet, quick hands, quick reaction on the part of the post man, thus helping to prepare him for the pressure of "pushing the ball towards the middle of the court" in the half court team defense.

Another ability the post man must have in this type of defense is the ability to block the shot or to take the charge. An excellent drill to teach these is described in Chapter 3—the REACT AND BLOCK DRILL. A quick recap of the drill will demonstrate how it forces the post man to make a quick decision on whether he can block the shot or should try to intimidate the shooter or get in the path of the driver and take the charge. All of these become crucial if the coach decides to influence the offense towards the middle of the court in his half court defensive strategy.

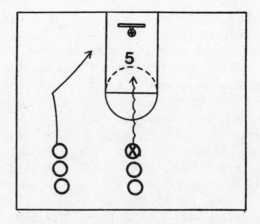

Diagram 13.5

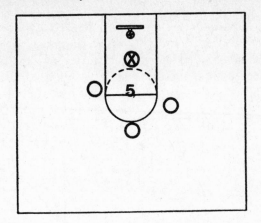

Diagram 13.6

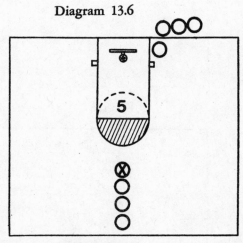

Diagram 13.7

React and Block. This drill is designed to increase the post man's foot and hand reaction while helping his skills in shot blocking. It also helps to teach "drawing the charge." The drill is set up as shown in Diagram 13.8. #5 is the post man, while numbers 1-2-3 are other squad members, each holding a basketball. A basketball is placed on the second free throw lane marking as shown in the diagram. The drill begins when player #1 rolls his basketball toward the free throw line opposite. (See Diagram 13.9.)

As soon as the ball begins to roll on the floor, #1 goes chasing after it. The rolled basketball MUST hit the free throw line as shown in Diagram 3.9. As soon as #1 has rolled the ball on the floor, the post man slides across to the BOX (first free throw marking), touches that with his foot and slides up the lane to swipe with his hand the basketball placed near the second lane space. In the meantime, #1 has picked up his basketball and now drives in for a layup. The post man, after swatting the basketball on the floor away, reacts to try to either block #1's shot, or get in front of him for the charge. Diagram 13.10 shows #1's path and #5's path.

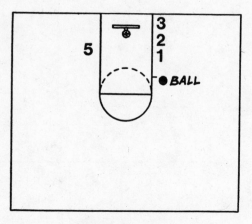

Diagram 13.8

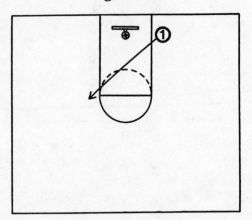

Diagram 13.9

This is an excellent drill and serves many purposes. Besides the obvious reaction on the post man's part, conditioning is a necessary result as we usually make the post man go through the entire team before he retires from the drill.

The post man must know how to take the charge, as many drivers will be coming his way down the lane. In the CHARGE-HUSTLER drill (described in Diagram 13.11) O1 starts with the basketball anywhere

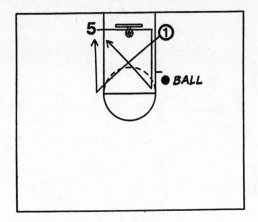

Diagram 13.10

along the court. The post man, X5, acts as the defensive man. #1 has just two rules of instruction to follow: (1) he must dribble drive around the chair, which is stationed about 4-5 feet from the baseline; so, he must drive between the chair and the baseline; (2) he must shoot a layup, no jump shot. X5 the defender knows what #1 must do. As #1 starts his dribble, X5 can stay close to him or can simply run down to the end line and station himself there, because #1 cannot do anything until he turns the corner between the chair and endline. Obviously, as a coach, you would not want your defender to do the latter.

The ultimate is the dribbler turning the corner and going between the chair and baseline, with the defender waiting there for him to take the charge. The pivot man must plant both feet solidly and position his arms in a natural defensive position—not protruding way out or back up against his chest. The defender should have his knees in, not protruding out, his base should be wide, and knees flexed. The post man has to be taught how to absorb the impact of the charge so that he is not hurt and is also taught to grunt loudly as impact occurs.

If the coach wishes to add more aggressive elements to the drill, he can, after the defender has fallen to the floor and taken the charge, roll a basketball toward the free throw line and make the defender scramble up and dive on the floor to secure the loose ball. Then, after scrambling to his feet, he picks up the ball and drives to the other end of the court where he shoots five power layups.

All of these drills can benefit every player on the squad. However, the post man benefits more than the rest because of the strategic position he holds down on the court and because he is the focal point of any defense, but particularly the defense described in the last few pages:

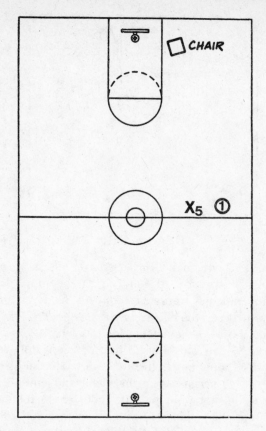

Diagram 13.11

a defense which channels or pushes the ball toward the post man in the middle of the court.

If the post man is not as co-ordinated, strong, and agile as you would like him to be, then perhaps your half court defensive strategy should be one of pushing the ball away from the middle of the court and forcing it wide at all times. Often an inexperienced post man or slow-reacting post man feels and plays more relaxed when he knows that his teammates are trying to keep the ball out of his area of the court. Pushing the ball wide involves a great risk along the baseline. An old axiom of basketball has always been: DON'T ALLOW THE OFFENSIVE PLAYER TO DRIVE BASELINE. Well, in pushing the ball wide, your team will be forced to push the ball towards the baseline. Diagram 13.12 shows the basic defensive alignment when the ball is out front at the guard position. Note that the strong side forward does not overplay his man as he did when the ball was being pushed to the middle. Now, the defense wants to encourage the ball to stay wide on the perimeter of the court.

When the offensive forward has the ball, in keeping with the general defensive strategy of pushing the ball wide, the defender overplays slightly in such a manner as to influence the forward to think that the baseline is open. Diagram 13.13 shows this maneuver.

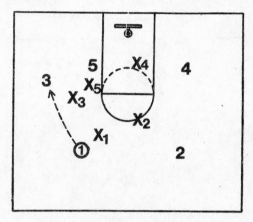

Diagram 13.12

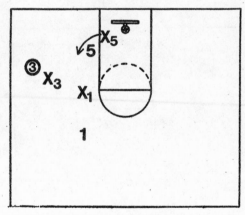

Diagram 13.13

Offensive forward #3 is thus encouraged to move toward the baseline. In trying to describe in words what the strategy is to be, it is best to tell the defensive forward to "push the ball *into* the baseline but don't surrender the baseline drive." Theoretically, the baseline becomes a sixth defender for the defensive team. The post man's main job in this defense is to be ready to cover baseline should the forward need help and to double team and trap along the baseline if the opportunity presents itself for such a maneuver.

The post man still has to be intelligent and agile, but not as much as in the previous defense of pushing to the middle. His basic area of coverage is greatly minimized in the defense which pushes the ball wide. As shown below, the post man's coverage area in a defense which influences the ball to the middle (Diagram 13.14) is greater than one which influences the ball wide (Diagram 13.15).

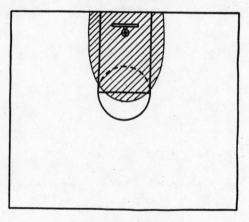

Diagram 13.14

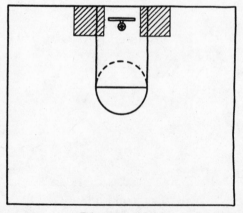

Diagram 13.15

Again, none of this is possible without the other members of the team being schooled in the art of defense. No matter if the team defense is a man or a zone, each squad member must know the basic strategy and be able to execute good sound defensive fundamentals.

In teaching the defense which influences wide, several drills are effective. A one-on-one drill starting from the sideline near the baseline can help a defender get the feel of driving his man into the baseline but not allowing him to go all the way to the bucket. See Diagram 13.16.

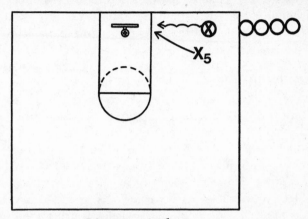

Diagram 13.16

A two-on-two drill using a guard and forward can be utilized to get across the idea of channelling wide. See Diagram 13.17.

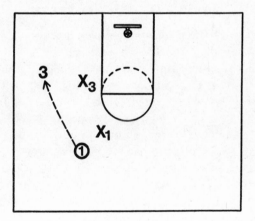

Diagram 13.17

And finally, a post man can be added to each of the above drills in order to teach the center the timing that is necessary to determine whether or not a fellow teammate has lost his man and needs help along the baseline. After all, the first principle of defense is TO GUARD THE BASKET. Hence, any time a dribbler loses his defender along the baseline and heads for the basket, the post man should be there to block his path.

Another alternative—perhaps a compromise alternative—to half court defensive strategy with the post man is the "COMBINATION" theory of defense. This theory combines the two previous theories. It emphasizes pushing the ball wide when the ball is above the free throw line extended, and then pushing it back out or towards the middle when the ball is below the free throw line extended.

On the surface this may seem like the most logical of the alternatives presented herein. But the disadvantage of such a system lies in the fact that the team has two alternatives to follow and must be especially cognizant of where the ball is on the court in relation to the free throw line. Often this causes confusion and indecision on the part of the defense. But if it can be mastered, it might be the best half court defensive strategy. Theoretically, the ball is kept on the perimeter of the defense. It is not allowed to go along the baseline. And the post man does not have undue pressure on his shoulders.

All three of these defensive ideas or strategies are based on team concepts. They all demand that coaches instruct their players how to "help and recover," how and when to "double up" on the ball, and how to play one-on-one defense.

INDIVIDUAL POST DEFENSE

As far as individualized, one-on-one post defense is concerned, there are only four ways that a defensive post man can play his offensive counterpart. The offensive post man may be sided from the baseline side of the court. He may be sided from the high side or free throw line side of the court. He may be fronted. Or he may be defended by standing directly behind.

The latter—playing directly behind the offensive post man—is sure death. No matter what the size of the offensive post man or what his ability happens to be, any defender who stays behind will either foul or give up many easy baskets. Nowadays, post players are too skilled and team offenses too sophisticated to allow such a defensive tactic to be employed without taking advantage of it.

Fronting a post player by positioning oneself directly in front of him is risky against a good team that knows how to attack such a maneuver. When a post player is fronted (as shown in Diagram 13.18), the defending team leaves itself open to the lob over the top for an easy score or a "swing" move by the offensive post man into the middle for a quick layin or short jumper. (Diagram 13.19 shows the swing move.) The only way these moves can be stopped is for the defense to be so aggressive on the ball that the passer is forced into making a poor pass or weak-side defenders react so quickly as to disrupt the flow by a steal or taking a charge.

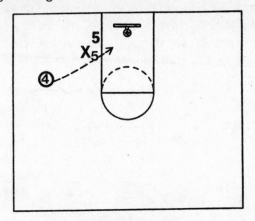

Diagram 13.18

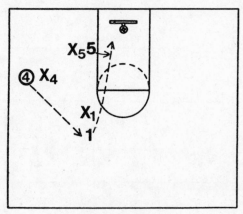

Diagram 13.19

There are times when it will be absolutely necessary to completely deny the ball to the post man by completely fronting. Such a situation usually occurs when there is a physical mismatch in the post area—when your post man is 6'3 and the opponent's is 6'11. Then to prevent the dominant post man from handling the ball, fronting is the best alternative.

But for most defensive situations, the best individualized way of guarding the post man is to "side" him. The basic rule of defensive post play is an old adage: BALL-YOU-MAN. The post man should stay on a direct line between the ball and his man, with himself between the two. The only variation occurs when the ball is positioned at or above the free throw line or below the free throw line. When the ball is at or above the free throw line, the defensive post man should be in a BALL-YOU-MAN position on the HIGH SIDE of the post man. Diagram 13.20 shows this. When the ball is below the free throw line, then the defensive post man should be in a BALL-YOU-MAN position on the LOW SIDE or BASELINE SIDE. Diagram 13.21 indicates this.

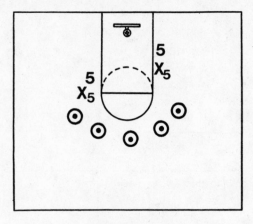

Diagram 13.20

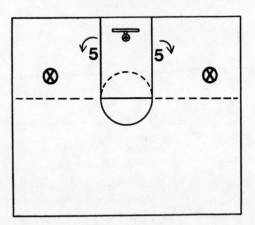

Diagram 13.21

The stance of the defensive post man is very similar to that of other defenders. He must maintain a wide base and keep his knees flexed so that he can react and move quickly. His head should be on the offensive man's chest with an arm outstretched into the passing lane. It is very important for the defender to lean the side of his head and ear into the chest of the offensive post player. This serves several purposes, including a distracting effect upon the offensive player. The defensive post man must be active and must beat his man to position on the court. He must read and anticipate. Not only must he concentrate on his individual man but, as indicated previously, he must fully comprehend the total team defensive strategy of pushing the ball to the middle, pushing it wide, or a combination of both. This forces him to react to the other four players on the court. The defensive post player has no easy task. That is why he is the most important man on the court for both teams.

In drilling the post man on his defensive techniques on the ball, it is important to over-exaggerate the situations because there will be slippage in the game. Therefore, forcing the post man to over-extend himself in practice will usually pay dividends in the games. Diagram 13.22 shows the post man reacting to three offensive players, two of whom aren't being guarded. Offensive players #1 and #3 cannot move from their spots but may pass the ball back and forth, forcing the post man to change his positioning following the BALL-YOU-MAN PRIN-CIPLE. Adding a third and then yet a fourth offensive player will add to the intensity of the drill. Any number of drills can be thought of to create post defensive situations like the one described above.

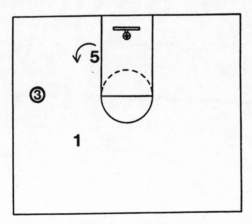

Diagram 13.22

Should the offensive post man get the ball, the defensive post man must play him according to the general team defensive strategy. If the entire team philosophy has been to push the ball into the middle of the court, then when the offensive post man receives the ball at the middle post his defender must take great care to make certain that he does not barrel to the basket down the lane. Rather, the defender must push the offensive post man to the center of the court where his teammates are there to help. Again, the basic first rule of defense is to GUARD THE BASKET and then prevent the LAYUP. Making the offensive post man shoot a turn-around jumper, a hook, a fade-away, *anything but* a power layup is a must for the good defensive post man.

Generally when the ball is pushed into the post man along the lane, bad things are going to happen as far as the defense is concerned. Team defenses have to sag or sink toward the ball when it is gotten inside by the offense. Thus, the defensive post man is usually given some help when his man has the ball. Previous chapters explained the basic offensive techniques used by the post man after he receives the ball. The offense in such a situation always has the advantage. The defense must be smart enough to hamper the offensive player in his attempt to get the easiest shot possible. GOOD DEFENSE is basically distraction of the shooter and preventing the easy layup. Post players must concentrate on these principles at all times.

In talking about defensive post play away from the ball, it is important to remember the "ELONGATED TRIANGLE" rule. This rule simply states that the defensive post man, when his man is away from the ball, should be at the point of an elongated triangle, the base of which is a direct line from the ball to the offensive man. This ELONGATED TRIANGLE PRINCIPLE is shown in Diagram 13.23.

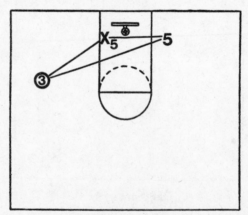

Diagram 13.23

In the diagram offensive player #3 has the ball. The post man is #5, away from the ball. X5—the defensive post man—is one step off the line of the ball (or the base of the triangle) and at the top of the triangle. Being one step off the line of the ball better helps to prevent a lob pass across court to the post man and usually forces the offensive post man to come "high" to receive the ball rather than "low." In coming high, the defense has a better chance to follow the principles of sound defense—in other words, guarding the basket and preventing the easy close-in shot. If the defensive post man were on the line of the ball (as shown in Diagram 13.24), he would be more susceptible to back door cuts and lob passes cross-court.

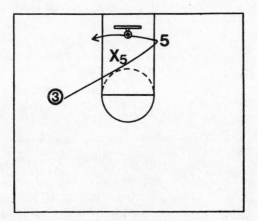

Diagram 13.24

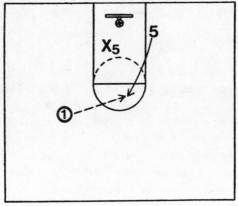

Diagram 13.25

In breaking down the weak-side post play even more, it is safe to say that when the offensive post man is on the weak side of the court, you should always make him receive the ball above you. If the ball is out front at the guard position, make the offensive post player come to the free throw line area to receive the ball (Diagram 13.25). When the ball is below the free throw line, make the offensive post player cut

above you to receive the ball. See Diagram 13.26. Forcing the offensive
post man to make these moves will result in him having to take poorer
percentage shots.

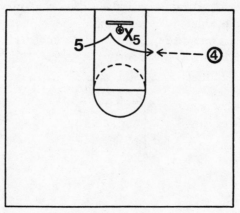

Diagram 13.26

All of these ideas can be worked on in practice by setting up drills
that simulate these situations. Remember that it is wise to make the
drills more difficult than they will be in game situations because of
game slippage caused by the internal and external pressures of the
game. But only by constant daily work can the post man become the
type of defender that will solidify the entire team defense.

HELP SITUATIONS

No matter what team defense you decide to employ, the post man
will ultimately become the last line of that defense. He is closest to the
basket on offense, and closest to the basket on defense. And though the
post man has to be able to stop the offensive post player, he must also
be able to stop any thrust towards the basket by *any* player on the
opposing team. He must literally be able to "guard the basket" no matter
what his size, ability, or agility might be. For this reason, it is mandatory
that you work continuously with your pivot players on "help" situations.
These are the situations that will test the post player the most. These are
the situations that occur most frequently in game competition. These
are the challenges that the post man must overcome in order to make
his team a successful one.

You have a crucial decision to make in regards to the post man
when "help" situations arise. Is the post man to automatically switch
off on the penetration to the basket? Or is he to stunt and help but
recover to his man? Knowing your personnel, knowing the ability and

agility of the post man will help you make this decision. Also, your basic philosophy on switching will come into consideration.

Whether there will be a complete switch on the dribble-penetrator or a simple stunt or help and recover, the drills will be the same. The post man must be able to stop dribble-penetration from the guard position. All of the drills described in the next few pages should be run first with the post man as the only defensive player going against two or three offensive players. Secondly, they should be run with an equal number of offensive and defensive players but always designed so that the offense has the advantage. Diagrams 13.27 and 13.28 show this, with 13.28 allowing the offensive guard to have a step on the defensive guard.

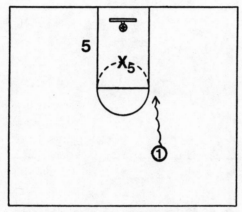

Diagram 13.27

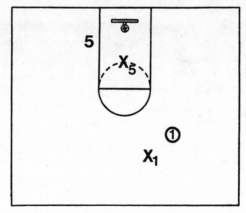

Diagram 13.28

Communication is so important in any "help" situation. If you get your players to yell "HELP" when they need it and the help-side players to yell "SWITCH" or "STAY" (depending on what you want the team to do in the situation) miscues will be minimized.

The same type of drills should be run from the wing or forward areas and from the baseline too. This will give the post man a chance to play the dribble-penetration from every possible angle. And coaches should not forget to work on help situations from the double low post area. Many teams run a double post or a high-low post situation. Diagram 13.29 shows this.

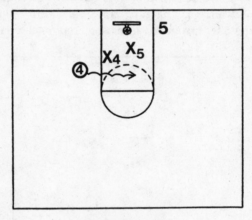

Diagram 13.29

In the diagram, #4 has posted up on the left side of the court. Assume he has beaten his man toward the middle, forcing the post man X5 to "help" out. Again, your half court defensive game plan and strategy on switching or staying will determine the exact nature of the defensive move. But, nonetheless, the post man does have to recognize and react to the situation.

Many offenses, especially those coming under the label of motion or passing game offense, utilize the post man as a screener. You must work on defensing moves whereby the offensive post man screens ON the ball and screens OFF or AWAY from the ball. One can either switch completely on such a move or STAY on such a move. Your basic philosophy of defense will determine the maneuver. Either way, it must be practiced over again to be executed flawlessly.

THE POST MAN AND SHOT BLOCKING

Because of the tendency for officials to protect the man with the ball or the shooter, it is very difficult to block a shot cleanly in the game of basketball. By "blocking a shot cleanly" is meant not only rejection of the basketball by a defender but gaining of the ball by the defensive team. Many shots that are blocked are either whistled as fouls or end up out of bounds and in the possession of the team that originally had the ball.

With these ideas in mind, it is often prudent to encourage players *not* to try to block shots but instead to try to distract the shooter as much as possible. But there will be certain situations when an attempt at a block shot is necessary. It might be the end of a game and mean the difference between a loss and a win. One might have a great height advantage over the driver to a basket. Or similar situations. If the decision is made to teach shot blocking, a few fundamental ideas are necessary.

The defender attempting to block a shot should never get into the direct path of the shooter. This would encourage contact and end up with a foul. When the offensive man is driving in from the left side for a left-handed layup, the defender should be on the side of the driver and use the right hand—the shooter's opposite hand—to try to block the shot. If the offensive player is coming in from the right side, then the defender would use the left hand to block the shot.

The shot blocker should be instructed to point the shoulder of his blocking hand at the driver. This forces the body to turn and again minimizes contact. The ball should never be blocked until it leaves the shooter's hand. And, if executed properly, the ball should be blocked back towards mid-court not out of bounds where the offensive team will still retain possession. After these generalizations, timing and practice are necessary.

The shot blocker should not try to block every shot. He has to be selective, utilizing his knowledge of his own ability and that of the man with the ball as regards jumping, finesse, strength and the like. Sometimes the defender should fake as if he were to block the shot and then pull back. This has a disruptive effect on many shooters. Sometimes it is wise to act as if you were going to block the shot and suddenly get into the path of the on-rushing dribbler to take the charge.

Above all, it is important to realize that shot-blockers are not plentiful in the game of basketball today. This is why the technique of blocking a shot should be taught with discretion by the coach.

SELECTION OF A TEAM DEFENSE BUILT AROUND THE POST

Mention already has been made of three possible half court man defenses built around the post player. But what about zone defenses?

The best type of zone from which to push the ball into the middle at a good post man is the 1-3-1. The post man is stationed in the middle of the second line of the defense. From this position he is in good shape to challenge penetrators at the middle and also have support from behind should the post man fail to stop penetration. The 1-3-1 zone is also adaptable so that the ball can easily be pushed wide and toward the baseline if you so desire.

But a far more effective zone at pushing wide is the 2-1-2 zone defense. This zone allows for more stunting and support by defenders while at the same time allowing for a clogging effect in the middle. If the post man is small and not as agile, this zone will better protect the middle and keep him from making a lot more defensive plays beyond his ability.

No matter what defense is selected, no matter what method of individualized defense is to be played by the post man, no matter what drills are incorporated into the building of a defensive system, the basic rules of simplified defense remain the same:

1. Guard the basket.
2. Guard the ball.
3. Don't let the offense throw the ball where they want to.
4. Keep a hand up on the shooter for distraction.
5. Don't foul.
6. Don't give up the second shot.
7. Make the opposition beat you with the jumper.

Following these seven cardinal principles will result in success.

14

AGGRESSIVENESS— COMPONENT TO VICTORY

Webster's dictionary defines "aggressiveness" as the "disposition to dominate." Coaches should like that definition. Everyone wants to dominate the opposition on both ends of the court. In the defensive end, every team's objective is to force the opponent to do what the defense wants it to do. Every defense wants to be so aggressive that the offense is under their control—that the offense is afraid of the defense. Fearless hustle from all players at all times, no matter what the score, is a team trait and individual trait that can be taught and achieved.

Offensive aggressiveness centers around the idea or concept of *attacking.* Styles of play may differ. But if the offense is constantly looking toward the basket and thinking "score"—whether it be in a fast break style of play or controlled, slow style of play—then pressure and the tendency to dominate is placed squarely on the defense.

It must be emphasized here that clean play and aggressiveness within the rules go hand-in-hand. Meeting with the squad, carefully explaining and emphasizing the rules of the game, can go a long way towards better play. While everyone cannot be quick, or big, or strong, there is absolutely no reason why each player can't be well-schooled in the rules of the game and why he can't be extremely aggressive. There is no reason whatsoever why every one of the players on your team cannot try to dominate the opposition.

MENTAL DEVELOPMENT

It is one thing to preach aggressive play, but quite another thing to get it. Before the physical development of aggressive play can be imparted, a mental development or transformation must take place. Player conferences at which time you can convey to the player your philosophy of aggressive play can take place formally or informally, in your office or in the hallway, at lunch time or at practice.

Having each player write down three personal goals and three team goals and then talking about these with the individual player is another way the coach can create an opportunity to emphasize aggressiveness. If the player's goals are not aggressive or forceful enough the coach can point this out to the individual and change them. This is also an opportunity for you to make "development of aggressiveness on defense" one of a non-aggressive player's personal goals.

The bulletin board is an effective place to preach aggressiveness. Slogans, pictures of players diving on the floor for loose balls, statistics and the like can help encourage aggressiveness.

Sometimes, depending on the individual player and his personality, reverse psychology can be used to develop aggressiveness. Although this is not the normal procedure, with certain individuals chiding or criticizing the lack of aggressiveness can lead to a development of aggressiveness. Pointing out the lack of aggressiveness in a sarcastic manner will at times show results. But coaches should be cautioned to use discretion in this approach. If used on the wrong individual, it can cause disastrous effects and a damaging relationship between player and coach.

Your enthusiasm and interest in all phases of a youngster's life can help lead a youngster to simulate that feeling in his own life and play. Organized practices, thorough scouting reports, the heaping of praise and levelling of desired criticism in practices can convince the youngster that you care and deserve the youngster's fullest co-operation. "Whatever the coach asks of me, that's what I'll give" is a most desirable attitude to have the player hold.

DRILLS TO DEVELOP AGGRESSIVENESS

Numberous on-the-court drills can be used to develop aggressiveness. None of these should be designed to inculcate fear in the player, nor should they be so rough as to incur injury. All of these drills should be scrutinized by the coaching staff so that they do not get out of hand. Aggressiveness, not recklessness, should be stressed.

Loose Ball Drill. The team is divided at both ends of the court as shown in Diagram 14.1. The coach is at center court and lays the ball on the floor. As soon as the ball leaves the coach's hands, the players at the front of each line rush for it. The one who gains possession is on offense, the other on defense. They now play 1-on-1. The contact in this drill is minimal, yet the philosophy of "going to get the loose ball" and "not being afraid of hitting the floor to do so" is inculcated. Basketball is a contact sport and conditioning an athlete to that contact—to the knocks and blows of individuals and the floor—is part of our job as coaches. Never toss the ball in mid-air. This forces players to go up in the high, much like soccer players do in order to head a ball. This is too risky and greatly increases the chance for injury.

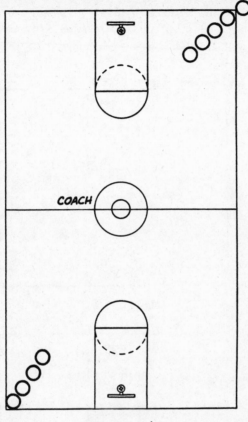

Diagram 14.1

Save the Ball Drill. This drill is designed to minimize the fear of saving a ball as it is about to go out of bounds, while at the same time creating a "designed play" that enables the team to actually return the ball in bounds safely to a teammate. Players should be instructed to never save a ball going out of bounds under their defensive basket unless a teammate is there to pass it to. How often have you seen a ball saved, only to be handed right in to an opposing player who lays it in the basket for an easy two points? The drill is set up as diagrammed in 14.2.

The coach, standing in the middle of the court, has a basketball. He flings it towards the out-of-bounds line in either direction. Player #1 or #2 have to get air-borne, secure the ball while in mid-air out of bounds, look in bounds and pass it to one of their remaining teammates. If at all possible, the teammates should come towards the ball in a direct line with the man saving the ball out of bounds. Diagram 14.3 shows the entire drill. Notice how player #2 moves over in a direct line with #1. As player #2 gets himself in position to receive the ball, he is instructed to yell "HERE" as a verbal signal to his teammate that he is in position.

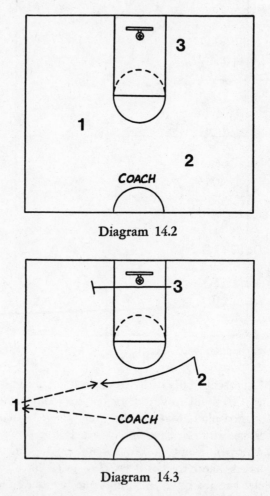

Diagram 14.2

Diagram 14.3

Back-Check Drill. Will your players literally "fly through the air" to poke the ball away from a player who has stolen the ball and is on a solo breakaway downcourt? This trait is a sure sign of aggressiveness and it can be developed. Line the players underneath one basket. The first player steps out to the free throw line. He is thrown the ball and takes off downcourt to try for a lay-up. The next player in line at the end of the court takes off after him and tries to hit the ball from the dribbler from behind. In most cases, assuming the players are of comparable speed, it can only be done by leaving one's feet and diving headlong for the ball. The drill is also a good one for the offensive player because he is forced to shoot the lay-up with the pounding thuds of the defensive man chasing him from behind.

Charge Drills. Being able to take the charge and being *willing* to take the charge is a sure sign of a tough, hard-nosed, aggressive player. Several charge drills have been mentioned previously in the book. The CHARGER-HUSTLER DRILL is described fully in Chapter 14 and the REACT AND BLOCK DRILL in Chapter 3.

2-on-1 Rebound Drill. This is a drill which many coaches probably already use. Three players are stationed around the bucket and a shot is taken. The three then battle for the ball. The player who secures it goes back up with it, as the other two try to stop him. No dribble is allowed. Play usually gets somewhat rugged. This is an excellent conditioner also, and it greatly encourages second, third, and fourth effort. Any number of players can be added to the drill. But the player that frequently comes out of the pack with the ball is going to be an aggressive player for you.

Mismatch Drill. This drill is designed to take a very aggressive player and match him up 1-on-1 against a not-so-aggressive player. So that the action takes place inside, start the 1-on-1 game at the low post along the lane, with the offensive player beginning with his back to the basket. Sometimes, to create even more aggressiveness, don't allow the offense to dribble. Players will have to take the ball up strong to the basket. If you have a post man who is not aggressive, match him up against a strong forward who is.

Fight-Back Layup Drill. This drill is set up in the following manner. Two players or student managers stand on either side of the basket. The player with the ball starts at the free throw line. He must dribble-drive down the lane and shoot a power layup on the right side. As he goes up for the power layup, the manager or player (who is holding a football fight-back hand dummy) gets one swipe at the shooter. As a coach, you must control the vigor of the swipe, not allowing the drill to get out of hand. After the player makes the layup, he dribbles back to the free throw line, dribble-drives to the opposite side, and repeats the lay-up there. Again, the student manager or player on that side of the court has one swipe with the hand-held fight-back at the shooter. Making the player score five layups on each side is usually enough to arouse an aggressive feeling or two in your shooter. The drill serves the purpose of making the offensive player take the ball up tough to the basket and also conditions him to body contact and makes him more aggressive.

No Foul Scrimmages. Without specifically stating it, the coach can often encourage aggressive play by allowing his players to scrimmage and not calling many fouls. For example when a player goes over the back of a defender and secures a rebound, the coach can praise the offensive rebounder for his action. In fact, this was a foul, but was not called. The next time down court the defender might be more aggressive on his block out or might go to the boards better on offense, knowing that you, the coach, praise such action when done by a teammate.

It is very important to note in all of these "aggressiveness" drills that the coach must exercise restraint and control. He must constantly preach clean and fair play and make sure that tempers remain calm and controlled. The purpose of the drills is to develop a spirit of "domination" in the athlete—a spirit whereby the athlete feels that he can control his opponent and have a confident attitude of playing against him.

MEASURING AGGRESSIVENESS

At times it is very difficult to measure aggressiveness, particularly *effective* aggressiveness. Oftentimes foolish aggressiveness leads to fouls and silly turnovers resulting in defeat. Players need some recognition for aggressiveness, especially on the defensive end of the court. Perhaps a set of defensive charts and statistics is the answer.

A defensive form can be employed which gives points for defensive plays. For example, a player who creates a turnover receives a +2. A player who dives on the floor (a very aggressive action) receives a +4. A player who takes the charge—a +5. Coaches can devise their own standards and categories. If the coach desires, he can also deduct points for failure to execute proper defensive fundamentals, penalizing the athlete more for lack of aggressive action. For example, failure to screen out on the boards might cost the player a —4. Failure to dive for a loose ball could cost a —5. Failure to jump switch properly, a —3.

If such a system is used, it might be wise to *only* display *these* statistics to the players after a game. If you are trying to encourage defensive aggressiveness, then the coach must show by his actions that defense is more important than offense. Instead of allowing the players to check their offensive stats after a game, *only* allow the defensive stats to be brought into the locker room.

Since the post man is the hub of both the offense and defense, every coach would like this player to be his most aggressive. It should be interesting to check the post player's plus and minus defensive points should the coach decide to keep these. A post player who leads his team in "taking the charge" and "diving on the floor for a loose ball" is one who will make his team a winner.

15

PRACTICE SECRETS AND
EVALUATION HINTS

POST MAN AND DAILY PRACTICE

Since the post player demands so many techniques and skills, he must be accorded plenty of individual attention during the practice sessions. The coach and/or an assistant coach should have or share the responsibility for working with the post players daily. Players who most often will pass the ball in to the post player in the team offense should work on these specific skills with the post man during practice. Timing and reading each other are very important in the total development of team play. For example, if, in the designated team offense, the forwards are the ones who constantly pass the ball into the post player, then they ought to be the ones throwing the ball inside in the practice drills. If, for instance, the coach wants the post player to work on his power moves from the middle post, then the forwards ought to make the pass inside so that the post man can power down the lane. Diagram 15.1 shows this thought.

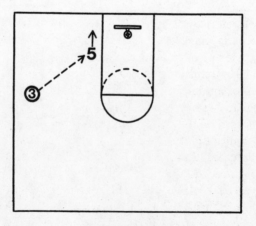

Diagram 15.1

Should the coach want the guards to work on their weak-side flare shot off the post man's pass, then a guard is added to the drill and is the receiver of the post man's pass. This type of teamwork is essential if game timing is to be effective. Diagram 15.2 shows the flare by the guard.

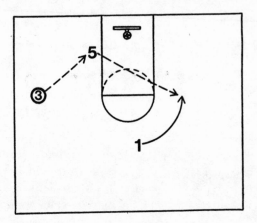

Diagram 15.2

If the post man is to work on his outlet passes to begin a fast break, then it would not be practical for him to throw the ball out to a student manager or a coach. Rather, have a guard, who is the outlet receiver, make his move to the area and work on receiving the pass from the post man. Using your players and, specifically, the players who will be working with each other in game conditions—using them together in practice drills—is the best way to develop the timing that is so essential to successful offense.

The post player is the one player who could most use pre-practice or post-practice extra time. Asking the post player or players to spend fifteen minutes prior to official start of practice or fifteen minutes after the end of official practice working on his positioning, his short hooks, his outlet passes, or power layups is not out of order. This is especially true if the post man has been made to think of himself as the focal point of the team, the hub of the wheel, the player around whom the offense and defense is built. Again, the idea of having a teammate stay and assist is more practical that having a coach make a pass or receive an outlet. If two are needed to work on a specific skill or technique, make that other player be a player—not a coach, assistant coach, or student manager. The coach, assistant coach, and student manager do not take the court and play against the opponents on game nights!

DAILY GOALS: 1. development of simple defensive maneuvers
                2. rebounding and conversion
                3. beginnings of offensive floor balance

Spartan Basketball Tradition

HEAD COACH: RICH GRAWER

STATE CHAMPIONS: 1973, 1978 and 1979
STATE FINALISTS: 1977, 1980
STATE QUARTERFINALISTS: 1971, 1974

WEEK: #2

SPARTAN BASKETBALL PRACTICE PLAN #   10

DATE   MONDAY, OCTOBER 30, 19

. . . .

3:15 - 3:16 ... flexibility

3:16 - 3:20 ... 2 man full court passing: good angle cut

3:20 - 3:25 ... 5 man delay cuts: meet the pass
                                    face the basket

3:25 - 3:45 ... shooting and individual work — POST PLAYERS
                                    with Coach Grawer
                                    —positioning, catching, power

3:45 - 3:50 ... defense agility: "CONVERT"

3:50 - 3:55 ... HEAD ON CHEST DEFENSIVE DRILL
                                    GUARDS - Coach Burgman
                                    FORWARDS - Coach Grawer
                                    POST MEN - Coach Boehm

3:55 - 4:00 ... 1-on-1 defense from BASELINE

4:00 - 4:05 ... 2-on-2 PUSH — INFLUENCE TO SIDE

4:05 - 4:15 ... 3-on-3 NOW PLAY

4:15 - 4:20 ... 4 baskets: OFFENSIVE REBOUND SEQUENCE:
                OTHER PLAYERS: 1 vs 2 ball-handling

4:20 - 4:25 ... 3-on-3 rebounding and CONVERT

4:25 - 4:30 ... REACT AND BLOCK DRILL — Post Players on DEFENSE

4:30 - 4:40 ... GUARDS: SCREENING POST/FORWARDS - posting up and
                Coach Burgman   hitting the post - Coach Grawer

4:40 - 4:55 ... HALF COURT OFFENSE: 4-on-4 PASSING GAME OFF
                                    1-3-1 set

4:55 - 5:10 ... BREAK SCRIMMAGE: 5 vs 4 with all four defensive men *up*

5:10 - 5:15 ... RUNNING AND SHOOTING 3 PLAYERS, 3 LANES

Post-Practice: POST MEN stay with two guards and
                work on pass, reception, and flare move

Not only for the post player but for the sake of the entire team, planned practices utilizing every second are essential to the development of a sound program. Before the start of the season, the coach should be able to break down his four or six week practice schedule prior to the first game, listing what he hopes to stress and accomplish during each week. It is often too much to plan daily practice schedules more than a week in advance. But setting weekly goals is not outlandish. For example, during the first week of practice (the first six practices) the coach might want to emphasize the fast break, establishing the method of making the outlet pass and the primary wave of attack with the front three players. He might also want to stress screening techniques and emphasize defensive ways of guarding the basket against 2-on-1 or 3-on-2 situations. It might not be until the second week that the coach decides to implement the beginnings of a half court offensive pattern against the man defense. Or not until the second week that the coach wants to teach the manner by which the team will handle the screen on the ball.

Once the weekly goals have been established, the coach can begin to make out his daily practice schedule for that week. The daily schedule should include three specific goals for that particular day. The schedule should make specific assignments for the assistant coaches and allocate specific times for each drill or technique. No drill should last more than 10 minutes. Most should go only about 5-7 minutes. Players get bored very easily and practices and drills must be varied. The key to success in basketball is repetition. But repetition for repetition's sake becomes non-productive if it is boring. So making a practice plan and daring to be innovative or different in that plan is a challenge to every coach.

Drills designed for the post man have to be particularly varied. Since the post man has so many things that he must master, developing different drills that ultimately teach the same thing is a necessity. Again, repetition that becomes boring also becomes non-productive.

Notice in the sample practice plan several items. First, the practice plan is made up for a two-hour workout. This is long enough for today's athletes to work, provided that during the two hours they do work and *work hard*. Second, the drills that are designed to go longer than ten minutes usually require a five minute orientation or explanation talk by one of the coaches. Third, at the end of the schedule is a post (after) practice session with the two starting guards and the post man and the coach. This will last for no more than five minutes.

A few other points of interest are in order. The head coach should meet with his staff for 15 minutes during the day to go over the practice schedule, making sure that each coach fully understands each item. A copy of the practice schedule is also given to the student manager. His job in practice is to be the official clock-watcher. He has a whistle and when the time for a specific drill is up, he blows the whistle signifying to all that the drill is over. A reliable manager is a must for a successful program. Also, if the two hour practice time is up, the players are instructed to walk off the court should the coach try to extend the official team practice. This philosophy keeps the coach on his toes and forces him to re-think each practice plan to get maximum usage out of the allotted time.

As mentioned before, when players report to the gym for practice they are instructed to work in pairs. Players never shoot by themselves when another player is in the gym. In keeping with general defensive principles, a hand in the face of the shooter in practice greatly aids in developing this trait for game conditions. And finally, silence is to be maintained at all times when the players hit the court. If they wish to talk to their friends, they should do it in the locker room. If they want to reminisce about a party or night out, they are to do it in the locker room prior to coming up to the court. This may sound harsh, but it is effective. With the silence that is demanded of the players, a lot of instruction can be done on the court. Players may talk during drills or scrimmages to convey to a teammate that they are open or that a certain play is to be run. That is not considered idle chatter or talking; that is considered communication—basketball communication. With the two hour limit that we place upon ourselves in practice, this silence rule is a must.

A breakdown of the particular practice plan shown on the sample would be very similar to all practice breakdowns. Approximately twenty-five minutes or about 20% of the practice time is spent on direct shooting. Twenty minutes are devoted to fundamentals—in this case, cutting, passing, and ten minutes of rebounding drills. Another 20% of the practice time is allocated to defense. And the remaining 33% or one-third of the practice time is devoted to team offensive concepts. It stands to reason that shooting and team offense should be emphasized, because these are the more difficult phases of the game, as they directly involve timing and the basketball. Twenty percent of the allotted practice time spent on defense is very workable, since defense does not have to worry about handling the basketball; and timing—especially team timing—is less essential.

As mentioned earlier in the book, conditioning is a two-way responsibility. Each player has an obligation to have himself in fairly good condition when he reports for practice on the first day. That is why we run the physical tests described in Chapter 2. Running for the sake of running is not done. Drills that combine conditioning aspects along with dribbling, passing, and shooting are a major part of any basketball program. And a two hour practice limit that moves at a frantic yet exact pace is in itself a great conditioner.

STATISTICAL EVALUATION OF
THE POST PLAYER

Coaches who keep game statistics usually keep the number of field goals attempted, number of field goals made, number of free throws attempted, number made, offensive and defensive rebounds, assists, fouls, and turnovers. Some coaches will keep a shot chart to determine where each player has shot from on the court. And some coaches keep defensive statistics in order to determine how many times a player dives on the floor after a loose ball, takes a charge, allows his man to go baseline, fails to block out, and the like.

Statistics can be a tool or they can be a crutch, depending upon how you view them. In dealing with the post man and trying to evaluate his play in your total scheme of play, a number of statistics are unusually revealing.

Just knowing how many times the post man has touched the ball off a pass by a teammate might indicate to you how much of a part the post player is playing in the offense. How many shots and from where taken is very important in determining whether the offense is being run as it is supposed to be run. The number of times that the post man has been fouled (not just the number of times that he goes to the line) is also an important tool in helping the coach determine whether or not his post player is effective. The number of rebounds the post man gathers is a logical statistic to keep; but how many coaches keep the number of outlet passes that the post man attempts—those that are successful, those that are not successful? If you are a fast break team, such a stat is very important to the success of your style of play.

Besides the post player's own statistics, it is often very useful to keep the opposing team's post man's stats: the number of shots that he takes, the number of shots made, where he made them, the number of times he touches the ball in their half court offense, the number of rebounds he gathers and the ensuing successful or unsuccessful outlet attempts, the number of assists he gets, and the number of times he gets fouled. These stats are helpful in evaluating your post player's defensive effort for a given game.

Such defensive stat sheets are very simple to make and an assistant coach or even an observant student or student manager can keep them.

If a coach really wishes to zero in and help his post player become the best player he can possibly be, then video-tape just his actions during a practice or game. Forget about the rest of the team. Have the video person concentrate on the player's movements up and down the court, in the offense and on defense. Some interesting things can be learned from such an endeavor.

No statistic can measure what is inside of a player—his spirit, his attitude, his morale, his effort. The coach knows this. Subjective evaluation by the coach with his player can best assess these items.

And finally, it is obvious that society measures basketball success in wins and losses. Rarely will a successful team—successful in victories—be weak in the pivot area. Rarely will a successful team lack an effective post player around whom revolves the offense and defense.

EPILOGUE

The game of basketball has seen changing trends to match the changing times. The 1-3-1 offense, the 1-3-1 half court trapping defense, the passing game, the match-up defense—these are just a few examples of trends that have come to the game of basketball and been adopted by coaches throughout the country because of the success of a championship team. Coaches are great imitators. Coaches are always looking for that little edge to make them champions. If a team wins a championship using a certain system on offense or defense, you can bet that such a system will become the "in-thing" during the next season for many, many teams.

Systems—offensive and defensive—do change from time to time. Variables in this game are many. However, in most systems, there is usually one constant. That constant is the idea of using a player or several players to work in the multi-purpose area—the key, the lane. Defense is built around the principle of guarding the basket. Offense is built around the principle of getting the ball in as close to the basket as possible to enhance scoring success. With this in mind, the post man has become crucial to the success of any team.

Realizing the importance of the post man to winning championships, you must devise a program and a system to develop that post man to his fullest ability. Such a system must be total and comprehensive. It must include off-season and pre-season work. It must include specific drills to develop agility and reaction. It must include a breakdown of the components of operating in the post area: positioning, giving a target, catching the pass, the move, the shot, the follow-up, the conversion to defense. The program for the post man must be specific in regards to the fast break, to the half court offense against both the man and the zone defense, to the delay game, and to the press attack. Such an offensive program is the nucleus around which to build other parts of the basketball program.

This book has been an attempt to supply the coach with some secrets in developing such a program. The ideas presented here are not meant to be exclusive of other post play ideas. They are, however, meant to stimulate thought and analysis. They are meant to encourage you to evaluate your current views on the game and to challenge you to review your system of post play—if you have a system.

It is true that the guards bring the ball up court and that forwards usually are the players who score the points and get the headlines. But the post player is the one who reaches out and meshes the four other players into a "team," mainly by his central location on the court. Do you know the SECRETS OF WINNING POST PLAY BASKETBALL? Having read this book, you are on your way to answering that question with an emphatic "YES."

Index